ON THE TRACKS OF OO7

You Only Live Twice

50th anniversary

Guide to Japan

by
Martijn Mulder

ISBN: 978-90-813294-0-8

Published by
DMD Digital

CONTENTS

Introduction – by Norman Wanstall 4

Country and Culture 7
Weather, Money & Electricity 9
Shrines & Temples 12
Cuisine 15
Some general do's and don'ts 16

Welcome to Japan, Mr Bond 19
Fleming's journey 19
The Making of You Only Live Twice 22
The art of ninjitsu 50
The Man With The Red Tattoo 54

Tokyo 56

Kansai 77
Toyota 77
Kyoto 81
Nachisan 85
Kobe 90
Himeji 91

Kyushu 99
Nagasaki 100
Kirishima 106
Kagoshima 114
Akime 122

You Only Live Twice - Locations scene by scene 145

Credits 170

INTRODUCTION

Having worked on EON's first four James Bond films, I was looking forward to the making of *You Only Live Twice* with great expectations. My editor Peter Hunt, who had contributed so much to the success of the series, was promoted to 2nd Unit director and the highly accomplished Lewis Gilbert, with so many successful credits to his name, was hired as director for the first time. The script was the first to bear little resemblance to Fleming's original story, although the ninja training school and Blofeld's piranhas survived, as did Bond having a Japanese makeover and Tiger Tanaka being head of the Secret Service. Kikumaru Okuda was hired as technical adviser, as the Japanese locations were certainly going to be the most challenging.

Before production started, Lewis and his Production Designer Ken Adam searched various Japanese locations in the hope of finding a seaside castle to match the one in Fleming's story. Unfortunately they were not successful, but whilst in a helicopter flying over Mount Shinmoe they developed the idea that perhaps the villain Blofeld could conceal his activities inside a volcano. This was incredibly ambitious, but the idea took hold and the result was probably the most incredible engineering feat in the history of films. The final set was the result of 379 conceptual drawings and was constructed by 250 craftsmen of every skill and trade. Those of us who were working at Pinewood Studios at the time spent every spare moment visiting the site to see how the set was progressing. Later when I was hired as sound editor on the film, I admitted that creating the sound of the rocket entering and leaving the volcano was the greatest challenge of my career.

The crew began shooting the film at Pinewood Studios, but they then left for Japan and spent several days on location work at the southern seaport of Kagoshima. After that it was on to the southern village of Akime for eight more days shooting and these were far more remote locations than had been used in previous Bonds. Whilst in Japan,

Peter Hunt attempted to shoot the scene where Bond's Little Nellie autogyro is attacked by villains in their Hillier helicopters. The cameraman shooting the scene was Johnny Jordan, sitting in a helicopter with his legs exposed and when one of the Hilliers rose up beneath him, the blades virtually severed his foot. He was rushed to a hospital in the village of Ebino, but sadly his foot had to be amputated back in the UK. The shooting of the scene was delayed, but eventually completed in Spain.

At the time the film was made, Bond films were very popular in Japan and Sean Connery's arrival at Tokyo airport was heralded by a fanfare from an all-girl brass band. He stayed at the Hilton Hotel and was hounded by both the fans and the press. Unfortunately the constant attempts to follow and photograph Sean, not only in Japan but also in Bangkok and Hong Kong, became too much for the actor and soon it became clear that he'd be unlikely to submit himself to the demands of another Bond shoot. He said that for him it was like living in a goldfish bowl.

Meanwhile the three Japanese actors were well cast and did an excellent job, but were all re-voiced in post-production. Clarity is essential for the world market and most foreign actors - including Ursula Andress - were re-voiced in the four previous productions.

One has to mention the contribution made by composer John Barry for his outstanding score. He composed the music for eleven James Bond films and his death in 2011 was a huge loss to the movie industry.

At the world premiere of *You Only Live Twice*, on Monday 12th June 1967, the Queen attended, which was the first time she'd been present at a Bond premiere. The film was a huge international hit and grossed $111.6 million worldwide in spite of not being quite the phenomenon that *Thunderball* had been. The film was certainly a joy to work on.

Norman Wanstall
Sound editor on *You Only Live Twice*
Oscar® winner 'Best Sound Effects' for *Goldfinger* - 1965
February 2017

COUNTRY & CULTURE

Japan is situated in north-eastern Asia between the North Pacific and the Sea of Japan. The area of Japan is 377,944 square kilometres, nearly equivalent to Germany and Switzerland combined or slightly smaller than California. Japan consists of 6,852 islands, including the three main islands: Hokkaido (northern island), Honshu (main island) and Kyushu (southern island).

There is only one official language spoken in Japan, which is of course Japanese. However, many Japanese are able to understand English to a certain extent since English is the foreign language that everyone must learn as part of compulsory education. Even if you don't understand Japanese, you can still certainly enjoy Japan. But if you know a few everyday Japanese phrases then it will make your trip even more memorable. A few words can make a big difference:

English	Pronounced	Written
Hello	Konnichi wa	こんにちは
Goodbye	Sayonara	さようなら
Yes	Hai	はい
No	Iie	いいえ
Excuse me	Sumima sen	すみません
How are you?	Ogenki desu ka?	お元気ですか？
I'm fine	Genki desu	元気です
Thank you (very much)	Arigatou (gozaimasu)	ありがとうございます
You are welcome	Do itashimashite	どういたしまして
Toilet	Toire	トイレ
Exit	Deguchi	出口

Japan's population is over 126 million. Most Japanese reside in densely populated urban areas. Japan's capital city is Tokyo. The population of the Tokyo Metropolitan Area is approximately 13 million. Looking at the other cities in this guide, Kyoto has 1.5 million inhabitants, Wakayama 370,000 , Nagasaki 450,000 and Kagoshima 600,000.

Besides the many islands, Japan has a lot of forests as well. The forests of Japan cover about 25.12 million hectares, which adds up to roughly 66% of the entire national land area. This means that Japan has one of the largest forest coverage rates in the world. Other areas used consist of 5.04 million hectares of agricultural land, 3.06 million hectares of other land, 1.74 million hectares of residential land, 1.33 million hectares of water surfaces, rivers, and channels, 1.23 million hectares of roads, and 260 thousand hectares of wilderness areas.

Japan's topographical features include coastlines with varied scenery, towering mountains (often volcanic) and twisted valleys that invite visitors into the mysterious world of Japanese nature.

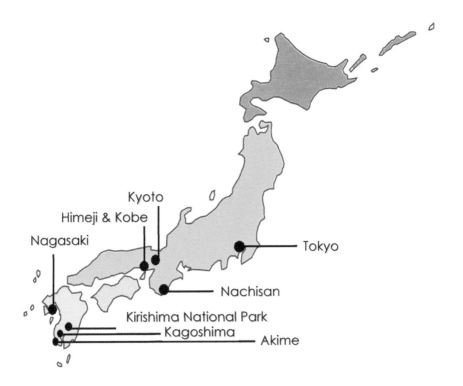

Weather

Japan has four distinct seasons. The climate can widely vary, depending on the region you visit, as the country is long from north to south. Honshu and Kyushu have extratropical climates, Hokkaido has subarctic climates, and the most southern, smaller islands such as Okinawa have subtropical climates. For example, springtime skiing can be enjoyed in the northern areas between March and April, but sea bathing can be enjoyed during the same time of the year on the islands in the southwestern areas.

Japan also has particular climactic events such as a rainy season and typhoons. Rainy days and cloudy days increase as the rain front becomes active from early June to early July in Honshu and from mid-May to mid-June in Okinawa. Cyclones over the Pacific Ocean intensify and sometimes pass near Japan from July to October. Statistics show that they move onshore the most between August and September. That would leave Spring as the best time to travel to Japan. In Spring, the average temperature in the cities in this itinerary, will be around 15 degrees Celsius (59 degrees Fahrenheit), so you should pack and dress accordingly. Light and comfortable clothes, with a light jacket will do.

Money & Electricity

The unit of Japanese currency is *yen*. Its currency sign is "¥" and is written "Yen" or "JPY" in foreign characters. Coins are available in denominations of 1, 5, 10, 50, 100 and 500 yen and bank notes in denominations of 1,000, 2,000, 5,000 and 10,000 yen. The smallest form of currency is the 1 yen coin, and the largest form of currency is the 10,000 yen bill. The 5 yen coin and 50 yen coin are rare worldwide in that they have holes in the middle of them. Please note that the values of all coins and bills excluding the 5 yen coin are written in Arabic numerals. Only the 5 yen coin has no Arabic numerals on it.

Consumption tax in Japan is 8%. Currently, whether indicated prices are tax-included or not is up to the store. Please ask the staff if the prices include tax or not, before making your purchase, if you would like to know how much you must spend.

There is no limit on the amount of any currency that may be brought into or taken out of Japan. However, if you transport (any currencies, checks, securities or other monies) exceeding 1,000,000 yen worth in Japanese currency into or out of the country then you must complete a customs declaration.

You can buy yen at foreign exchange banks and other authorized money exchangers. At the international airports, currency exchange counters are usually open during normal office hours. The exchange rate fluctuates daily depending on the money market.

Post offices throughout Japan are equipped with cash dispensers (ATMs). You can withdraw cash in Japanese yen from your bank account via an ATM using a debit cards/credit card issued in your country. All stores affiliated with the 7-Eleven chain of convenience stores and the AEON chain of supermarkets have ATMs as well. The International ATM Service sign and the logos of usable credit cards are displayed on the machines. The ATMs at 7-Eleven stores allow you to withdraw cash 24 hours a day, making them extremely convenient.

Do note that OTHER ATMs often DO NOT accept foreign cards!

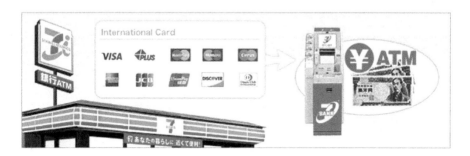

TIP: The "Japan ATM Navigation" app by Seven Bank is a convenient way to use your smartphone to navigate to the nearest 7-Eleven ATM. I strongly recommend you download, install and use it.

Credit, debit and prepaid cards of International brands are accepted by most hotels and merchants. There will be instances where merchants may not display the card acceptance marks so do not hesitate to ask the salesperson if your card is accepted. You can use cards for Narita Express (JR) and Shinkansen (JR) fares; however, you may not be able to use them to pay for most of short distance train/subway fares.

Travelers Checks are accepted by leading banks, hotels, ryokan (Japanese inns) and stores in major cities.

* * *

The voltage in Japan is 100 Volt, which is different from North America (120V), Central Europe (230V) and most other regions of the world. Japanese electrical plugs have two, non-polarized pins, that do fit into North American outlets.

Japanese power outlets are identical to ungrounded (2-pin) North American outlets. While most Japanese outlets these days are polarized (one slot is slightly wider than the other), it is possible to encounter non-polarized outlets in some places.

Some North American equipment will work fine in Japan without an adapter and vice versa, however, certain equipment, especially equipment involving heating (e.g. hair dryers), may not work properly or even get damaged. If you intend to purchase electronic appliances in Japan for use outside of Japan, you are advised to look for equipment specifically made for oversea tourists.

The frequency of electric current is 50 Hertz in Eastern Japan (including Tokyo, Yokohama, Tohoku, Hokkaido) and 60 Hertz in Western Japan (including Nagoya, Osaka, Kyoto, Hiroshima, Shikoku, Kyushu); however, most equipment is not affected by this frequency difference.

Kiyomizu-dera temple overlooking Kyoto

Shrines and Temples

Japanese Shinto shrines and Buddhist temples are one type of sightseeing spot that attract a great deal of tourists from abroad. Shrines in the mountains with breathtaking scenery and temples with a beautiful melding of architectural structures and gardens in the traditional format are simply amazing to see. And these are also places that have been treasured by the Japanese people since days of old. Perhaps it is wise to learn the correct way to pray and enjoy a casual trip to some of these wonderful places.

First, let's take a look at the differences between shrines and temples. Shrines are built to serve the Shinto religious tradition, and are characterized by a *torii* gate at the entrance. Temples are built to serve the Buddhist religious tradition, and are characterized by a *sanmon* gate at the entrance. They exist side by side, without trouble.

Torii gate at Nachisan

Sanmon gate at Nachisan

Shrines:

1) Pass through the torii gate.

All shrines have a torii gate, which is considered the boundary line between holy ground and the secular world. Passing through the torii gate signifies that you have stepped into the domain of the deity. Though awareness of torii etiquette has dwindled recently, bowing once in front of the torii gate is the correct procedure. Also, the centre of the pathway entering into the shrine is considered the area where the deity passes. Key to a polite visit therefore is to avoid this centre space and to walk to the side area of the pathway.

2) Purify your hands and mouth at the *"temizuya"* water pavilion

The *"temizuya"* water pavilion consisting of a water basin and ladles is not a place to drink water. It is there to perform "misogi," a ritual to purify the body and mind with water before proceeding to stand in front of the deity. Originally this ritual was performed in the nude at special misogi locations like the ocean or a river, but today the ritual has been simplified to rinsing your hands and mouth at the *temizuya*.

- First, scoop up water in a ladle with your right hand and pour water over your left hand.
- Next, hold the ladle with your left hand and pour water over your right hand.
- In your left hand, take some water that you have scooped with the ladle and rinse your mouth. Never touch the ladle directly to your mouth.
- Lastly, using the remaining water, tip the ladle to rinse it off.

Note: You only scoop up water one time, at the very first step of the process.

3) At the altar, bow twice, clap your hands twice, and then bow once to pray.
The number of bows and handclaps may differ at some shrines.

Temples:

Temples do not have any one procedure for visiting that is as strict as shrines. If a temple has a *temizuya*, purify your hands and mouth in the same way you would at a shrine and head to the altar.

Do not clap your hands.

Temizuya, where one can purify the hands and mouth

Washoku

Cuisine

Washoku, which is Japanese cuisine with a culture that has its own unique place in the world, was added to UNESCO's Intangible Cultural Heritage list in December 2013 as part of the "Traditional Dietary Cultures of the Japanese".

Basic don'ts when enjoying Japanese cuisine:

- Disregarding how the dish is presented (such as eating stacked ingredients from the bottom).
- Bringing your mouth to your serving dish (please bring your serving dish to your mouth).
- Putting your elbows on the table.
- Eating directly from the platter when food is served on a platter (please place food on your own plate before eating it).

How to pour sake: Hold the bottle with your right hand and place your left hand on the lower part. This applies to all drinks you may be serving.

There is also etiquette to be followed by those being served. Please hold your cup up when having sake poured into it. This is the opposite of when being served wine. When you have had enough, please say so as you place your hand over your cup. You can also leave your cup on the table without finishing it all.

Some general do's and don'ts

- There are places where wearing shoes is forbidden. Taking off your shoes when entering the house is a common practice in Japan. This applies not only to houses, as there are many facilities such as temples, restaurants and bathhouses where shoes must first be taken off before entry as well. When entering a building, it is a good idea to first check and see if you are supposed to take off your shoes and wear slippers inside.

- Bargaining and tipping are <u>not done</u> in Japan. Leaving money on the table in a restaurant, will usually result in the waiter chasing you down the street to give it back (Which on the other hand might be an interesting and fascinating sight..).

- It goes without saying that tossing cigarette butts on the streets is forbidden, but there are many locations such as streets and public facilities where smoking is prohibited. Please smoke only in designated areas.

- In Japan, people greet each other by bowing. A bow can range from a small nod of the head to a deep bend at the waist. A deeper, longer bow indicates respect while a small nod with the head is more casual and informal.

  Bowing with your palms together at chest level is not customary in Japan. If the greeting takes place on tatami floor, people get on their knees to bow. Most Japanese do not expect foreigners to know proper bowing rules, and a nod of the head is usually sufficient.

  Shaking hands is uncommon, but exceptions are made.

- Kissing and hugging is not a common form of expressing emotions among Japanese people. However, Japanese people have respect for foreign cultures. Please interact with Japanese people in accordance with the culture of your country.

- Speaking on mobile phones should be avoided when using public transportation.

- Passengers should stand in a straight line when waiting for the train. The lines are formed at designated areas.

Info partly provided by the Japanese National Tourism Organization and Japan-guide.com

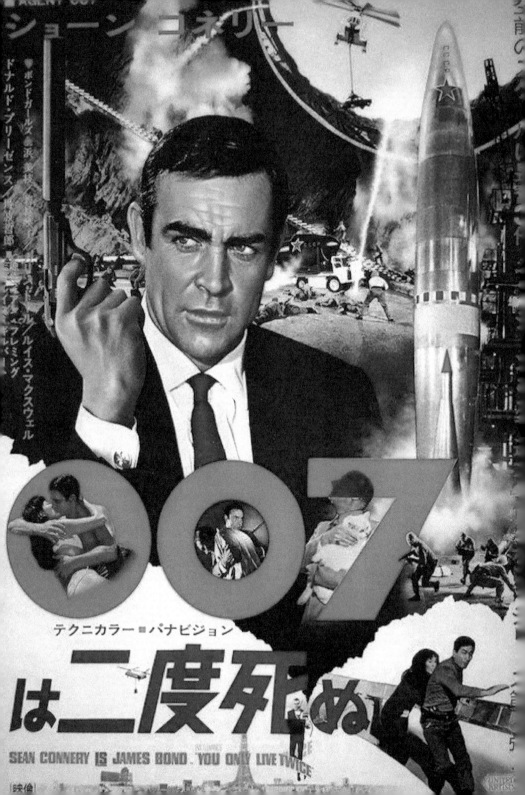

WELCOME TO JAPAN,

MR BOND

Of all the locations in the Bond films, Japan still stands firmly as the most exotic ever used. In my opinion at least. Back in 1966, it was definitely considered exotic. Unspoiled and unknown enough to send Bond there on his latest mission. Today, some 50 years later, these things can still be said of this beautiful country. Its cultural heritage, being so different, not only from the West, but different from the rest of the East as well, and a very turbulent history filled with samurai, kamikaze pilots and two devastating atomic bombs, make Japan one of the most interesting countries one can visit.

Fleming's journey

When Ian Fleming travelled the world, researching his *Thrilling Cities* travel stories, he also visited Japan, in 1959. Very impressed by the Japanese culture, he thought it would be interesting to bring 007 to this far away world. Therefore he returned to Japan in 1962. When the first Bond film Dr. No was about to be released, Fleming had already started writing this new novel, *You Only Live Twice*. It was to become the last one that was published before his death. Fleming had read books about Japan, but felt he needed to return to the islands. So he contacted his long-time friend Richard "Dikko" Hughes, an Australian journalist who had worked and lived in Japan for 13 years. Fleming instructed Hughes that he wanted to see pearl girls diving, hot baths, live volcano 'for suicides', and 'any manifestation of the horrific'. In his book *Foreign Devil* (1972), Hughes devoted a whole chapter to the trip he, Fleming and journalist/editor Torao "Tiger" Saito made for the development of Fleming's novel.

The trip took two weeks and started in Tokyo. From there, the three amigos took the bullet train to Gamagori, south of Nagoya, where they boarded a hydrofoil across the Ise Bay to the pearl diving island of Mikimoto. Next stop was Kyoto, where they visited the *Nijo Jinya* inn, with all its trap doors and secret passages. From Kyoto they went to Kobe, where they took a steamship to Beppu on the southernmost island of Kyushu.

On Kyushu they found Flemings 'live volcano' in Mount Aso. Their last port of call was Fukuoka, which Hughes later regretted. He stated that *Nagasaki would have been a far more interesting choice*. From Fukuoka they took the late night express back to Tokyo.

Hughes wrote that he and Tiger simply adjusted to Fleming's working technique. During the day the three men travelled, observed and made inquiries. Every evening before dinner, Fleming would leave the two men for two hours, to write down his impressions of the day and to draw up questions and anticipations for the following day.

It was during this two week trip, that Fleming constructed his haiku, attributed in the final novel '*after Basho*'. His first - and according to Hughes his best - attempt was:

You only live twice:
Once when you are born,
and once when you are about to die.

After returning to Jamaica, Fleming finished the novel, immortalizing both his travel buddies, as the characters of Dikko Henderson and Tiger Tanaka.

The novel was the last one in the so called 'Blofeld trilogy' and it picked up where the previous adventure, *On Her Majesty's Secret Service*, had left us: After having just lost his wife, Bond is in desperate search of Blofeld but cannot seem to find him. To get his mind off things, he's sent on a mission to Japan where, in an unusual twist of faith, he finds his wife's killer, walking around in a medieval harness in his castle's garden, surrounded by toxic plants. While this plot sounds a bit absurd, the novel is actually a very fine one and over the years has become one of my personal favourites. Truth is that it would have made a lousy film script, since it lacked the over-the-top action the cinema audience had gotten used to.

The Making of *You Only Live Twice*

When Cubby Broccoli and Harry Saltzman had finished the hugely successful *Thunderball*, their initiate decision was to have *OHMSS* as the follow up. In the early video releases, one could read "The end of *Thunderball*, but James Bond will return in *On her Majesty's Secret Service*", which was removed from later versions. But, since both stories heavily relied on large action scenes (compare TB's underwater action with *OHMSS*'s snow action) and problems with a warmer-than-usual Swiss winter and inadequate snow cover, the idea was dropped and the decision was made to start working on *YOLT* instead, thus reversing the original order of Fleming's continuing revenge story.

Editor Peter Hunt, who was promised the directing job on *OHMSS*, was extremely disappointed when Broccoli and Saltzman confronted him with their decision and needed a break from the series. When the producers offered him a paid vacation around the world, second unit direction on *YOLT* and the promise that 'his' film *OHMSS* would be the one after *YOLT*, Hunt fortunately agreed to return. Lewis Gilbert was offered the director's chair and together with the producers and production designer Ken Adam, the search for suitable locations was on and the team went to Japan.

Working with story outlines submitted by Sydney Boehm and Harold Jack Bloom, and armed with the itinerary of Fleming's journey with Hughes and Saito, the production crew (Broccoli, Saltzman, Gilbert, Adam, Bloom and Maurice Binder) went to Japan in February 1966, where they spent a month scouting possible locations.

They rented two helicopters and flew around Japan for two weeks, covering every square inch of coast, searching for the medieval castle Fleming had described in his book. Unable to find any castles in the coastal area (it later turned out the Japanese hardly ever built castles along the coast) the group went looking for other storyline options. It wasn't until they flew over the Kirishima National Park and saw the green crater lake of Mount Shinmoe (*Shinmoe-dake* in Japanese) that the idea of the volcano base began to emerge. The rest is history.

Shinmoe-dake in Kirishima National Park

23

Ken Adam made a few drawings of the volcano set, Cubby Broccoli asked what it would cost to build it, Adam roughly estimated *"One million dollars"* and Broccoli, without blinking his eyes, replied *"If you can do it for a million dollars you can start building it"*, giving the very talented Ken Adam the opportunity to create one of the most memorable sets ever designed.

Writer Roald Dahl was brought in to write the screenplay and he used several elements that were originally written in the first outlines, which he mixed with fresh ideas based on the locations they had found in Japan. In May, after Dahl had delivered a first-draft screenplay, they returned to Japan to further work out the story, look for additional locations and to cast the leading Japanese roles.

As a result of the collaboration with the leading Japanese Toho Studios, EON was forced to use local Japanese actors. Lewis Gilbert had worked with Tetsuro Tamba before, so he was an obvious (and excellent) choice to play Tanaka. For the female parts, many Japanese girls were tested, until they settled for two of Toho's stars, Akiko Wakabayashi and Mie Hama. Hama would initially play Suki, the agent who rescues 007 more than once, while Wakabayashi would play the island girl Bond marries to in order to complete his disguise.

Mie Hama, Sean Connery and Akiko Wakabayashi

The girls were flown to London, where they got a crash course in English. After a month it turned out Wakabayashi managed herself well enough, while Hama still struggled with the English language. Gilbert instructed Tamba to take the girl out to dinner and tell her she could no longer be in the film. When Tamba returned, later that evening, and informed Gilbert that Hama had threatened to commit suicide, it was hastily decided she would be fine in the film as long as she wouldn't speak much. Therefore, the girls swapped roles and Suki became Aki (played by Akiko Wakabayashi), while Mie Hama would play Kissy Suzuki, the island girl that marries Bond. Kissy had only a few lines to say and in the final film, Hama was re-voiced (like so many before her) by Nikki van der Zyl.

Casting was complete, just before filming started on the 4th of July 1966. Well, almost complete.. There was no Blofeld yet, but this would be taken care of in time, Gilbert was told by Broccoli and Saltzman.

Mie Hama at Shinmoe-dake

Tetsuro Tamba at Akime

Connery and Hama at Shinmoe-dake

The first three weeks, filming would take place at the Pinewood Studios just outside London. The first scene of the film was also the first scene that was filmed: Already part of Bloom's first draft, 007 was assassinated in Hong Kong and 'died on the job'. The following weeks, the interior scenes were filmed of Henderson's house, Osato's office and Tanaka's train office.

July 25th, cast and crew flew to Japan for a ten week period of location filming. After a few days of adjusting to their new environment, they went to the Southern island of Kyushu, where they used the Shiroyama Hotel in Kagoshima - then known as the Castle Park Hotel - as their home base. Scenes were filmed in the tiny fishing town of Akime and in and around Kagoshima itself. Early August, a small unit of cast and crew members started filming on top of Mount Shinmoe, where they were transported to every morning by helicopter.

Kobe docks was their next stop, where they filmed the scenes of Bond and Aki spying on the Ning-Po. August 20th the production went to the historical Himeji Castle to film the ninja training scenes. When the Japanese press falsely accused the production team of damaging the castle walls, Himeji officials quickly withdrew the filming permit. The crew then moved on to Nachisan to film the marriage between Kissy and Bond. Here in the mountains, next to the beautiful Nachi-no-taki waterfall, Connery celebrated his 36th birthday with the crew.

After this rural adventure, the production returned to Tokyo to film the remaining scenes in and around this bustling city.

Mid-September, the first unit returned to the UK, while Peter Hunt and his second unit stayed behind to shoot additional material that didn't require the presence of the main stars. Hunt filmed the ninjas climbing around Mount Shinmoe-dake, the black sedan being picked up by a magnet and 'dropped in the ocean' and of course the exciting aerial dogfight, with the film's big surprise: *Little Nellie*, the autogyro, piloted by its inventor Ken Wallis, who allegedly flew a total of 46 hours for just seven and a half minutes of screen time.

Wallis came from a family of aviation pioneers and by 1966 was a retired RAF Wing Commander. He devoted his post-military life to the autogyro, a small one-man helicopter he had designed himself and had first flown in 1959. Eventually, five autogyros (officially called *Wallis WA-116 Agile*) were built by Beagle Aircraft in Shoreham, UK, the majority for military purposes.

A BBC interview with Wallis was overheard by Ken Adam, who pitched the idea with Broccoli and Saltzman. Wallis was contacted and invited for a demonstration at Pinewood Studios, after which it was decided that the autogyro would be a great addition to the film. The special effects team started working on several ideas to fit the autogyro with machine guns, rocket launchers and missiles, much like the Aston Martin DB5 was gadget laden in Goldfinger.

Wallis' autogyro with the registration number *G-ARZB* was flown to Japan and Wallis himself was hired as pilot, doubling for Connery during the flight scenes. His army commander nicknamed the autogyro 'Little Nellie', after the British actress / comedian / dancer Nellie Wallace. According to Wallis this was common practice during the Second World War, when everyone whose last name was either Wallace or Wallis was called 'Nellie'.

Original storyboard drawings of the reconnaissance flight

31

The G-ARZB fitted with gadgets, posing on stage at Pinewood Studios. The Kagoshima street and volcano-background is a painting.

The crew encountered serious issues while shooting the aerial scenes. Since the autogyro was sprayed over, Wallis noticed his gauges were as well. He therefore had to fly using a stopwatch to be able to know how much time was left before he would run out of fuel.

On one occasion, while filming the appearing helicopter silhouettes around the slopes of Kagoshima's Mount Sakurajima, Wallis suddenly ran out of fuel. He was forced to land on a small mountain road, leaving at least one Japanese driver speechless.

The most famous incident occurred while filming the helicopter chase over the Kirishima National Park. Cameraman John Jordan, who was filming hanging half outside a helicopter, had his foot severed when one of the Japanese pilots flying an enemy Bell 47 helicopter directly below him, suddenly moved to a higher altitude. The helicopter's rotor blade had cut through Jordan's lower leg, so he was immediately rushed to hospital. Doctors initially managed to re-attach his foot, but sometime later, back in the UK, it turned out the foot had to be amputated anyway.

When it turned out the production team would not get permission to fire rockets and use explosives over Kirishima National Park, the decision was made to film the remaining part of the dogfight over the *Sierra de Mijas*, behind *Torremolinos*, Spain. Wallis was rather worried that the now fitted and working rockets would destabilize the autogyro. Additionally, test firing the rockets proved they were dangerously wobbly and seemed to have a boomerang-effect! So he personally went shopping for roofing lead, which he fitted inside John Stears' missiles as counterweight. This worked very well.

Connery filming the close-ups at Pinewood in front of a blue screen.
For these shots, a second autogyro was used.

Back in London, director Lewis Gilbert had other issues to deal with. While preparations had started to film the scene in which Bond and Kissy escape Blofeld and the exploding volcano, there was still nobody cast as S.P.E.C.T.R.E.'s number one.

Just as time was running out and Gilbert was about to give up, producer Harry Saltzman informed the team from Los Angeles that their Blofeld was on his way to London. He had singlehandedly cast Czech actor Jan Werich, who indeed arrived shortly after. Gilbert wasn't pleased with Saltzman's choice, but had no choice but to start working with the actor, who barely spoke English.

Gilbert's initial resentment proved correct, as Werich couldn't convince as Blofeld. Apart from his English (he would most likely be re-voiced anyway), he moved around very slowly and wasn't very menacing. When Werich fell ill after a week of filming, Gilbert convinced Broccoli and Saltzman that they should release Werich from his contract, because it simply didn't work. And so it happened. Werich went back home and the search was on for a new Blofeld. One of the few actors that was available on such short notice, was Donald Pleasance, who fortunately accepted the part.

Pleasance didn't look very menacing either, so it was quickly decided to give Blofeld a huge scar, that was in fact glued to his face. All Werich's scenes obviously needed to be reshot, but they made it all work. The scene in the control room, in which we see Blofeld's face for the first time, is very effective and a highlight of the film.

This page and opposite page: Jan Werich as Ernst Stavro Blofeld

Having fun on the set:
Connery and Pleasance (top)
in the control room, Connery in
his space suit (bottom).
Both scenes were filmed at
Pinewood Studios.

Donald Pleasance posing on set as Bond's archenemy Ernst Stavro Blofeld and in conversation with Sean Connery in between takes at Pinewood Studios.

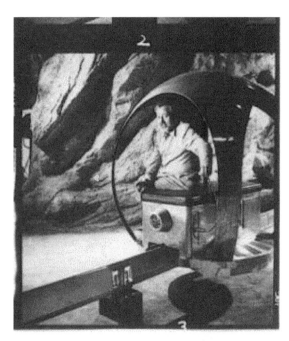

You Only Live Twice: same scene, two different actors. The top photo shows Jan Werich as Blofeld using the monorail in his volcano lair. The bottom photo shows Donald Pleasance in the same scene.

The true star of the film is of course Ken Adam, on whose magnificent interior volcano set filming commenced on October 31st 1966. A few days earlier, cast and crew celebrated the completion of the largest set ever built and the press was invited to have a sneak peek.

Lois Maxwell, Akiko Wakabayashi, Sean Connery, Karin Dor and Mie Hama

40

Sean Connery filmed his final scene, the fight with Blofeld's henchman Hans for the key to blow up the S.P.E.C.T.R.E space craft, between November 29th and December 2 and then he was done. Filming inside the volcano would continue until a few days before Christmas though.

In the new year, there were various crews working on different scenes, all over the world: Model work at Pinewood, underwater action in the Bahamas, a submarine in Bermuda, the fake funeral on board the *HMS Tenby* at Gibraltar and the remaining dogfight in Spain. Filming officially ended on March 30, 1967.

Maurice Binder returned to produce the main title sequence. With flowing lava as its main theme, Binder incorporated geisha silhouettes and Japanese style umbrellas, creating a visually stunning spectacle.

Previous page:
Top: Connery in between takes at the crater set
Bottom: Connery listening to Karin Dor, who played Spectre agent Helga Brandt

Below:
Connery in between takes with Tsai Chin, in the very first scene filmed for YOLT

John Barry was contracted to write the score and he produced some very elegant tunes that perfectly suited the mood of the film. Barry also wrote the theme song, after the producers rejected a Shirley Bassey-like rather bombastic theme song submission by soul singer Lorraine Chandler. The lyrics were written by Leslie Bricusse, who had previously co-written the lyrics for *Goldfinger*.

Above: John Barry giving notes during the You Only Live Twice recording sessions
Opposite page: Nancy Sinatra and John Barry at CTS Studios on May 2nd, 1967

Barry's first choice was British pop singer Julie Rogers, who recorded a slow version of the song with a 60 piece orchestra. This song later turned up labelled as 'demo' on the limited edition 2-CD *30th Anniversary Best of James Bond Collection*, even though Rogers at the time was convinced she recorded the final version of the theme.

The producers weren't convinced that Rogers' recording fitted the film, so Barry suggested Aretha Franklin to record it. Cubby Broccoli however wanted his friend Frank Sinatra to do it, and when Sinatra was contacted, he suggested that they used his daughter Nancy instead. Barry and Bricusse re-wrote the song to fit Nancy Sinatra's vocal range and by the end of April 1967 Nancy flew to London, accompanied by her younger sister Tina.

On May 2nd, they arrived at CTS Recording Studios and Nancy would later admit she was terrified that she had to sing in front of the EON producers and their wives, Barry & Bricusse, and about 60 professional musicians. After squeaking her way through a couple of takes, she felt so nervous that she even suggested to Barry that he could better call Shirley Bassey.

Eventually Barry offered to record the orchestra first, so Sinatra could record her vocals separately. After 30 takes, Barry was finally convinced he had enough material to choose from and in the end he used the vocals from 25 different takes to create the final product. When it was apparent that United Artists would not promote a single version of the song, Sinatra's own producer Lee Hazelwood recorded and produced a more up-tempo funky version, that even featured a double layer of Sinatra's vocals.

Back at Pinewood, Lewis Gilbert had brought in his own editor, Thelma Connell, who had already started working on the print. Connell had serious trouble with the pace of the film and with the action scenes in general. In the end she produced a rough cut with a running time of three hours. Unhappy with the whole situation, Broccoli and Saltzman asked Peter Hunt to help her out, which he did. As *supervising editor*, Hunt cut the film back to 117 minutes, pleasing both the producers and cinema operators throughout the world.

You Only Live Twice had its premiere at the Odeon Leicester Square in London on April 12, 1967, in the presence of H.M. the Queen.

By the time *You Only Live Twice* premiered, Connery was done playing 007 and had already announced this to the media while on location in Japan. His relationship with Harry Saltzman had deteriorated to the point where Connery stopped acting in the middle of a scene, the moment he spotted the producer around stage.

During the production, it is said Connery felt underpaid, 'partly to make up for the oppressive media attention had had received while on location in Japan'. While this might be true, Connery did receive five per cent of the net profits for his services to EON Productions and an additional five per cent of all profits the film made outside of Great Britain, Ireland and North America. Above this, he would receive a whopping 25 per cent of all profits received by Danjaq from the merchandising of the James Bond character and the 007 trademark, something he would later claim to have never received.

Whatever the case, Connery was largely unhappy during the making of YOLT and more importantly was afraid of being typecast in the future. Therefore he turned down the offer to play 007 in *On Her Majesty's Secret Service*, which would have been the last of the originally negotiated five separate options for subsequent Bond pictures after *Dr. No*. Instead, Connery left the franchise which had made him a star, to make a western with Brigitte Bardot.

Author Ian Fleming with producers Harry Saltzman and Cubby Broccoli in 1962

Artwork by Frank McCarthy

The promotional artwork was created by artists Robert McGinnis and Frank McCarthy.

While McGinnis came up with a new variation of the now famous Bond pose – complete with Walther LP-53 airgun – this time with Connery carrying a space helmet, he also designed the YOLT logo, with the word TWICE splitting up. He also contributed the bathing scene drawing, used widely throughout the world.

McCarthy focussed more on the action and came up with the exciting volcano attack painting, as well as the Little Nellie chase.

YOU ONLY LIVE TWICE

Artwork by Robert McGinnis

The art of ninjitsu

You Only Live Twice was the first film in which western audiences could have a good look at a wide number of martial arts techniques, normally only shown in Asian cinema.

The audience was introduced to the *ninja*, shadow warriors famous for their vast number of weapons and tricks. Ninja were the espionage agents and hired assassins of the great lords of Japan, hundreds of years ago. But including these visually interesting ninjas sounded easier than it was, since there were only a few authentic specialists in the art of *ninjitsu* in Japan. One of them was Yoshiaki Hatsumi (who would later change his name to Masaaki Hatsumi), who the production team had met during their first recce. Hatsumi had given them a demonstration of different kinds of ninjitsu weapons and the team was very impressed when they left. They promised Hatsumi to return in a few months and to consult him whenever possible.

The team had learned from Hatsumi that there wouldn't be very many people able to display ninjitsu, so he offered them to train stuntmen to do the job. So the search was on for athletic men, either stuntmen or men practicing martial arts. The team looked at teachers in all sorts of other styles as well and during a few weeks in 1966, you would have a hard time finding a black belt fighter anywhere in Tokyo, as they were all hired as ninjas by EON.

Still, Sean Connery had to get a crash course on the various martial arts that would be displayed in the film. The question who eventually gave these instructions is surrounded by much controversy, since three men claim to be responsible. Donn Draeger, a former U.S. Marine major - at the time living in Japan – was first hired by EON Productions to train Connery. According to Draeger, the actor showed a natural ability and quickly understood the logic of the basic offensive moves of stick-fighting (or *bojitsu*). Draeger choreographed some of the scenes at Himeji and even doubled for Connery in some of the fights. He awarded the actor a certificate in his American Stick Fighting Organization and accompanied him on a visit to another instructor, Masutatsu (Mas) Oyama, who claims to have been teaching Connery karate in privacy at the New Otani Hotel, before filming started.

Oyama, although born Korean, is considered a Japanese karate icon. Founder of *Kyokushin Karate*, the first and most influential style of full-contact karate, Oyama established his first dojo in 1953. By the time he died in 1994, he had built his International Karate Organization, *Kyokushinkai*, into one of the world's foremost martial arts associations, with branches in more than 120 countries boasting over 10 million registered members.

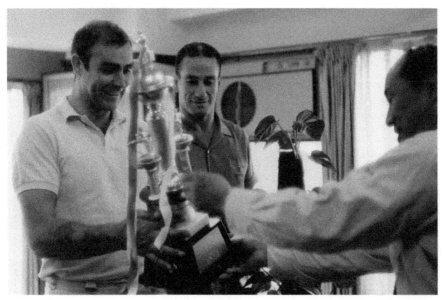

Connery is handed an award by Mas Oyama. Draeger observes in the middle.

When Draeger (who was one of Oyama's close associates) and Connery visited Oyama's Tokyo Kyokushin dojo, Oyama treated them to a spectacular demonstration and awarded Connery an honorary third *dan* in his organization. Once again, the martial arts world grumbled that such rank should be earned, and not handed to an actor for playing someone who knows karate. But, apart from these controversies, Connery had a wonderful time, as can clearly be seen in the pictures taken that day.

Connery and Mas Oyama, at the latter's dojo in Tokyo

A third instructor brought into the production is Shohitsu Nakajima, by many considered a walking controversy, as he claims to hold an almost impossible amount of high rankings in as many different martial arts. Nakajima can be seen in some of the behind-the-scenes photos of the ninja training scenes and many of his students were brought in as extras. He was also hired by EON to come to London. There he had the task of instructing all the UK stuntmen who had to perform as ninjas in the scenes shot at Ken Adam's volcano set at Pinewood.

Nakajima later admitted that many of the ninja-techniques used in the film were not authentic, but around 70 percent was. By many Japanese martial artists, this figure was considered to be 69 percent too high.

The Man With The Red Tattoo

In 2002 the 35th official James Bond novel was published. Written by Raymond Benson, *The Man With The Red Tattoo* marked the return of 007 in Japan. Benson had researched his book the year before during a trip with his friend James McMahon and included quite a few Tokyo-locations: The Meiji Shrine in Yoyogi Park, the Imperial Hotel, the Tsukiji fish market and the Great Buddha at Kamakura. But the main focus was on the arty Naoshima Island, halfway between the cities of Osaka and Hiroshima. Here, the Benesse House Art Museum was the location of the book's climax.

Naoshima embraced 007's literary adventure and saw an excellent opportunity to promote the area by making Benson ambassador of the Kagawa prefecture. They also initiated the establishment of the '007: The Man With The Red Tattoo Museum', which opened its doors in 2005.

The museum commemorates Benson's book and James Bond in general and is worth a detour, just for curiosity. Located in a small unmanned building, the museum is just a two minute walk from the ferry that brought you to the island. Among the many exhibits are notes and photographs collected by Benson, as well as a manuscript of the book, Japanese-style posters, postcards, model cars and guns, other 007 novels and other such movie paraphernalia.

The '007: Man With The Red Tattoo Museum' is located at 2310 Miyanoura, Naoshima-cho, Kagawa-ken. It is free to visit and open between 9am and 5pm.

The 007: Man With The Red Tattoo Museum on the island of Naoshima

TOKYO

Tokyo is a city forever reaching into the future, resulting in sci-fi streetscapes of crackling neon and soaring towers. This city is constantly reinventing itself – most recently as a culinary and pop-culture mecca. Yet it is also a city steeped in history. There are excellent museums here, along with everything else you might expect in Japan: Temples, shrines, palaces, gardens, architecture and hot springs.

During the Muromachi-period (1336-1598), Japan had politically fallen apart in many small regions, where local warlords or daimyo ruled. Based in Kyoto, Toyotomi Hideyoshi and Tokugawa Ieyasu, both followers of the important shogun Oda Nobunaga, planned and executed the unification of Japan. They decided the new capital of the country would be the city of Edo. At the end of the 19th century Edo was renamed Tokyo. At that time, the city was by far the largest in the world. Comprised from various smaller villages, the Greater Tokyo Metropolitan Area now houses about one fourth of the Japanese population. In an area of about 600 square kilometres, almost 32 million people live and work. This automatically means it can get pretty crowded during rush hours..

On September 1st 1923, Tokyo was struck by a massive earthquake, causing a great loss of lives. Since most of the buildings were made of wood, almost the entire city burnt down when large fires broke out. After the city was rebuilt, the recession and political climate caused Japanese Emperor Hirohito to choose the side of fascist Germany in WWII. Japan started its own war in the Far East and even attacked the U.S. at Pearl Harbour. The U.S. immediately retaliated and Japan was extremely heavily bombed. Most major cities were completely devastated, Tokyo included (only the city of Kyoto and its

Tokyo with the Tokyo Tower on the right

many important temples and shrines were spared) This partly explains the lack of truly old, historical buildings in Japan. When two U.S. atomic bombs forced Emperor Hirohito to capitulate, the Japanese population was left astonished and it took them decades to accept this defeat.

Once again, Tokyo was hastily rebuilt, without careful urban planning, and this gives the city a messy sight. Most visitors will arrive at Narita Airport, some 60 km east of the city. Narita was built to relieve Haneda Airport, which is west of the city.

Because Japan works with a very difficult address system (municipality + district + block number + house number which is not mentioned on the building itself), I will try to describe the Tokyo filming locations as best as possible and give you the nearest metro station (**M**) or train station (**T**).

TOP 5 PLACES TO SEE IN TOKYO:

1. **Tokyo Tower**
   At 333m the Tokyo Tower is 13m higher than its European counterpart, Paris' Eiffel tower. Marvellous views of the city!
   (M: Kamiyacho Station – Hibiya Line)

2. **Shibuya Crossing**
   It would be a shame to come to Tokyo and not take a walk across the famous intersection outside Shibuya Station. When the lights turn red at this busy junction, they all turn red at the same time in every direction. Traffic stops completely and pedestrians surge into an organized chaos.
   (M: Shibuya Station – most lines)

3. **Meiji Shrine (..Red Tattoo book location)**
   Dedicated to the late 19th-century emperor who opened Japan to the West, Tokyo's most famous Shinto shrine is wonderfully serene and less of a tourist trap than Senso-ji, the big Buddhist temple across town in Asakusa.
   (M: Meijijingu-Mae Station – Chiyoda Line)

4. **Yoyogi Park (..Red Tattoo book location)**
   Next to Meiji Shrine and the most entertaining green space in Tokyo, Yoyogi draws all sorts of talent, from horn players to hip-hop dancers to rockabilly gangs.
   (M: Meijijingu-Mae Station – Chiyoda Line)

5. **Shinjuku Gyoen National Garden**
   The most beautiful garden of Tokyo. English Landscape, French Formal, Japanese Traditional (with teahouse) and the curiously named Mother and Child Forest (Haha to Ko no Mori). There's also a lovely Taiwan Pavilion.
   (M: Shinjuku Station – most lines)

There are many options to get to the city centre, taking a taxi being the most expensive. You could take the train, or even better, take the Airport Limousine, a shuttle bringing you directly to some of the larger hotels. When you have to decide on a hotel in Tokyo, you would probably prefer to stay at the Hilton, which was the place Connery and the other main actors stayed, when they first arrived in Japan. That hotel unfortunately no longer exists. The original Hilton was demolished in 2008.

On its former location, you can now find a brand new Capitol Tokyu Hotel, a very fine hotel, located next to the *Hie* Shrine. This holy place was visited by Connery and his then wife Diane Cilento, followed by hordes of journalists, as can be seen in the episode of Whicker's World, dedicated to the making of this new Bond film. The episode painfully documented a lot of what caused Connery to quit the role of 007, even though he recognized it had brought him to stardom.

August 2, 1966: Press conference at the Tokyo Hilton

Since the original Hilton is gone, I can now really only recommend one place to stay: The Tokyo New Otani. Apart from it being one of the finest hotels I have ever stayed in, it has a definite James Bond connection, because it was a filming location in *You Only Live Twice* and it was the hotel where the other crew members stayed.

In 1966, the New Otani was just two years old and only consisted of one building, which was the tallest in Tokyo at that time. Its strange shape (three rectangular wings with a circular, revolving restaurant on top) made it an excellent choice for a Bond location and the fact that the hotel had (and still has) one of the most beautiful landscape gardens of Japan only added to this. The main building itself became *Osato Chemicals*, the exterior of the office building Bond forces his way into, to copy the contents of the safe and later in the film meets with Mr. Osato and his beautiful assistant Helga Brand. While all interior scenes were filmed at Pinewood, the exterior still looks exactly like it did back then. The stone columns outside the front door are still there, as is the large parking lot you can see Aki drive through several times in the film. The surroundings changed completely though.

Filming one of Bond's escapes on the New Otani parking lot

Two more towers were added to the complex in 1974 (Garden Tower) and 1991 (Garden Court), while the main building saw a major renovation in 2007. All these additions caused the disappearance of at least one filming location: The former southern exit. There used to be an elevated road, running from the main building towards the southernmost tip of the garden, where a curve brought the road back to street level. You can see this old street exit in the scene where Aki rescues Bond, when the latter visits Osato, while pretending to be Mr Fisher. Bond and Aki race off together, pursued by 'gunmen in black sedan' and use this exit to return to the streets of Tokyo .

60s postcard of the New Otani, showing the former southern exit (white arrow)

The New Otani landscape garden was also used as a location. This 400-year old garden was originally part of the residence of the Fushimi-no-miya family, the oldest of the four branches of the Imperial Family of Japan (before that, the land was owned by samurai lord Katō Kiyomasa). The later additions of buildings unfortunately caused the garden to shrink to its current size.

When Bond is chasing the thug who killed his contact Dikko Henderson, he can be seen running through this garden. After tackling the thug, a small fight takes place on a lawn with deer statues in the back. Most of this grass has disappeared. The deer statues are still present in the garden, but you really have to look carefully to find them. When you are walking through the garden, follow the path up hill to the garden restaurant. You should be able to find the statues when you stand in between the two buildings. They're almost hidden between the trees.

The historical tea ceremony house at New Otani's landscape garden

Deer statue hidden in the garden

Observing the waiting accomplice

In the film, after Bond has defeated Henderson's killer and put on the latter's clothes, you can see him hiding behind a tree, looking down some stairs, to find a waiting car. This scene was filmed at the west side of the garden, near the swimming pool, where similar stairs are still present. The waiting car was at the current Western parking lot.

It's funny to see the car leave the New Otani gardens, drive through the city, only to return to the New Otani entrance, now serving as Osato Chemicals HQ. The insert shot of the car driving through the city (with a 'wounded' Bond on the back seat) was done in the Azabu-juban municipality in district 2, on the one-way road between blocks 1 and 19 (Thanks to Thomas Gleitsmann for finding this!) (*M*: *Azabu-juban Station – Namboku Line / Oedo Line*)

In a strange twist of faith, the New Otani gardens would be re-used in another scene, later in the film. When the crew was filming the final scenes of the ninja training at Himeji, they were (falsely) accused of damaging the walls of the historical structure. This made the local authorities immediately withdraw the filming permit, leaving Lewis Gilbert with an unfinished scene. This scene, in which Bond was attacked by an infiltrated SPECTRE agent during his training, was later finished outside the New Otani. In the landscape garden, a bright red bridge brings you to the other side of the pond. With a historical tea ceremony house in the background, this beautiful setting can clearly be seen in the scene where Bond defeats his Himeji-attacker.

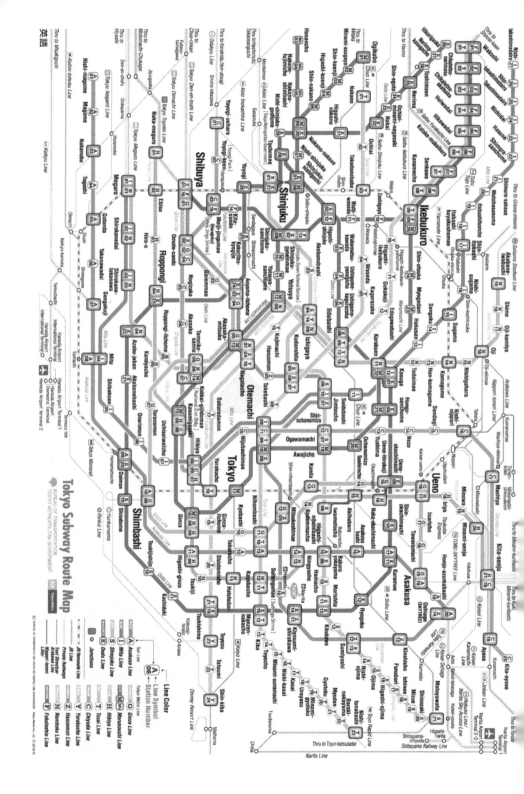

Tokyo Subway Route Map

BUREAU OF TRANSPORTATION
TOKYO METROPOLITAN GOVERNMENT

The New Otani Hotel is located near the large Akasaka-Mitsuke metro station, serving both the important Ginza en Marunouchi lines. Take the Marunouchi line (in the Tokyo metro system this is the red coloured line) in the direction of Ogikubo. After about 20 minutes, exit at Nakano-Sakaue (**M06** – note the capital M) and change to the smaller sub-line towards Honancho. Exit at **m05** (note the small m), which is Nakano-Shimbashi, and make your way outside to street level. This is the station used in all the metro station-scenes.

Nakano-Shimbashi station, pre 2014   Platform

Outside and inside this small and relatively quiet station the scenes were filmed in which Aki lures Bond to Tanaka's headquarters. The entrance to Nakano-Shimbashi undergone major renovations in 2014 and unfortunately no longer looks like it did when Aki parked her Toyota outside and ran inside. The interior is still recognizable though, especially the stairs and corridors.

The biggest change inside, is on the platform itself. Years ago, barriers were placed between the platform and the tracks, to prevent people from falling down. While this certainly takes away part of the charm of this location, it is still not very hard to recognize the place where Tanaka and Bond walked before they boarded Tanaka's own Secret Service train. All in all a nice location, away from the busy centre, and certainly not, as many sources state, in the heart of Ginza district! (This mistake is probably caused by the fact that there is also a Shimbashi Station in the Ginza district, only without 'Nakano-' attached,..)

69

Shibuya crossing at night

The next Bond location worth visiting can also be reached by metro. If you take the same Marunouchi line in opposite direction (either from Akasaka-Mitsuke or Nakano-Shimbashi) and get out at Ginza Station (**M16**), you will be in the exciting heart of Tokyo. Just take one of the many street exits from the station to enter the shopping and nightlife district that likes to compare itself with New York's 5th Avenue. Big designer stores will help you make your shopping experience an expensive one. The large neon signs on top of every building on every street corner surely make an impression and are always used in every film's establishing shot: "Welcome to Tokyo". They all look so familiar, it's like a constant feeling of deja-vu..

Like most city centres, the Ginza district has undergone massive changes and large shopping malls and designer stores have wiped out all the smaller shops visible in the street scenes in YOLT. When Bond has just arrived in Tokyo, we see him walk the streets of Ginza's 5-chome, through Miyuki-dori. Since the smaller streets and alleys have no name signs, it is almost impossible to give you any further directions.

Therefore you are encouraged to go look around for yourself using the map on the next page, to see if you can spot the alley where Bond walked into.

This scene was actually shot in two different alleys. The one where you see him walk into the alley is different from the alley where Bond walks through the door, that brings him to the sumo arena. The first alley is next to the *Mariages Freres Paris* tea house in Suzuran Street, while the second is a block away, in Miyuki-dori towards Namiki-dori. This same area is used when Bond and Aki are on their way by car to Henderson's house. But in this case it's an easy one, since the street name is clearly visible on screen: West 5th Street.

Ginza alley where 007 enters the beauty salon. *Bar Lupin* is still there.

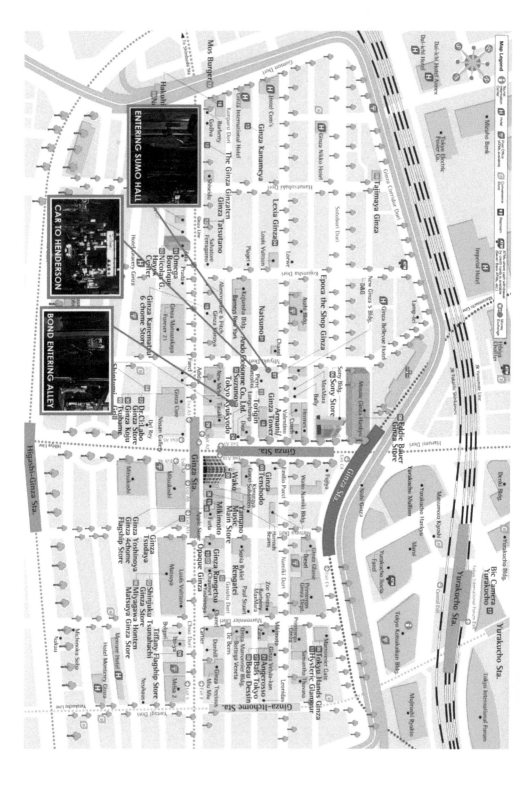

The sumo wrestling arena where Bond meets Aki, Kokugikan, was originally located in the Kuramae neighbourhood. Filming took place here in from 5 to 7 September, 1966. Since Allied Forces occupied and used the original wrestling hall after the Second World War, a new building was constructed in 1950. The interior of that building can be seen in the sumo wrestling scenes in YOLT. In 1985 a new wrestling hall was built at Ryoguku, after which the Kuramae Kokugikan was demolished. So if you like sumo wrestling you should visit the new Ryoguku Kokugikan. For Bond locations you can skip it. (*M: Asakusabashi Station – Asakusa Line **M16**)*

The location used for the exterior of Henderson's house has puzzled many for years. Even the local fans had big trouble finding this spot. Until someone stumbled upon one of the few remaining photographs of the place. It used to be a restaurant called Fukuhisa, located near the waterfront in Tokyo's Omorihon-cho district. Unfortunately this building no longer exists. (*T: Between Heiwajima Station and Omorikaigan Station – Keikyu Line)*

The final places of interest in the city are all connected to driving scenes. When 007 leaves Osato Chemicals, we see him walk towards the New Otani parking lot. A black sedan pulls up behind him, a shooter takes aim and Aki saves the day. Bond jumps into her Toyota and together they race off, followed by the gunmen's car. After exiting the hotel grounds from the earlier mentioned southern exit, we can see the pursuing car drive towards Benkei Bashi, the bridge over the Benkei moat that runs around the western and southern sides of the hotel grounds. (*M: Akasake-mitsuke Station – Ginza line* **G05** / *Marunouchi Line* **M13**)

The shots that follow were made in the Akasaka municipality, just south of the New Otani hotel. In the 6th district (chome), the cars can be seen driving around the 12th and 18th block. Although it's factually interesting, there's really not much left that resembles the 1967 film scenes. The only thing that still looks the same is the street layout. (*M: Akasaka Station – Chiyoda Line* **C06**)

An insert shot for the car chase (the one with the visible detour-sign) was made in the Higashi municipality. The cross roads used are just below the Hiroo High School, in Higashi's 4th district, block 14 (*M: Ebisu Station – Hibiya Line **H02***)

Suddenly the cars have left the urban development behind them and we see a few 1964 Tokyo Summer Olympics landmarks pass by. First we see the cars drive along Komazawa Dori, and speed past Komazawa Olympic Park (*T: Komazawa-Daigaku Station – Tokyo-Den-entoshi Line*). In the next shot we see them pass the Yoyogi National Gymnasium on the southern side (*M: Yoyogi-koen Station – Chiyoda Line **C02***).

The car chase ends 100 kilometres away, at Fuji Speedway in Oyama, Shizuoka prefecture. Originally designed to be a high-banked superspeedway for NASCAR-style racing, the race track opened in December 1965. Two months earlier, the Mitsubishi Company had taken over control, after the initial corporation ran out of funds. At that point, only one of the projected two high-banked curves was completed and the track was converted to a road course.

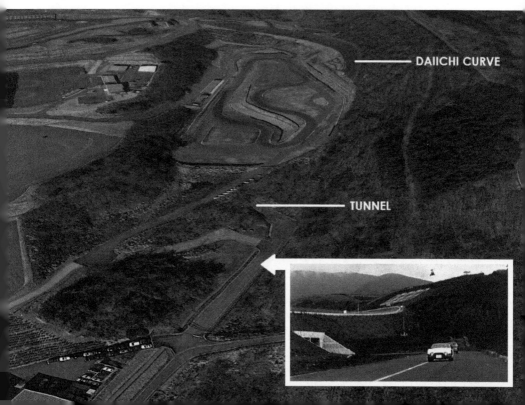

DAIICHI CURVE

TUNNEL

The large 30 degree banked curve (named "Daiichi") was kept in the track and can clearly be seen in You Only Live Twice. Aki and Bond, followed by the 'gunmen-in-black-sedan', appear from a tunnel (that comes from under the race track). At that point the helicopter appears from behind the surrounding mountains and the elevated Daiichi-curve can be seen on the left of the frame.

The banked curve regularly resulted in major accidents and after a double fatal accident in 1974, it was decided to shorten the track, abandoning the Daiichi curve. Fuji Speedway was acquired by the Toyota Company in 2000, after which more renovations and redesigning of the track took place. It re-opened in 2005.

While part of the abandoned Daiichi-curve is still visible, the tunnel has been closed (filled up) and the road Aki and Bond drove upon – and where the black sedan was picked up by the magnet - is now fenced off and not accessible for regular visitors.

KANSAI

For our next stop we leave Tokyo and travel south-westwards to the Kansai region. You can either take a domestic flight or travel by lightning fast Shinkansen. The latter will bring you from Tokyo to Kyoto in just 2,5 hours. Halfway you will reach another interesting stop for us.

Toyota

The current city of Toyota was originally called *Koromo* and used to be a major producer of silk. One of the most important families was the Toyoda family, with the great Japanese inventor Sakichi Toyoda as their head. After his death in 1930, the lack of demand for silk and cotton brought a recession to the area, forcing his son Kiichiro to sell their company's factories and to look for other opportunities. He decided to start making automobiles and founded the Toyota Motor Company, based in Koromo.

In 1959, Toyota had become the largest employer in the region and it was decided that the city of Koromo from then on would be known as *Toyota*. Unsurprisingly twinned with Detroit USA, the city of Toyota still houses the car manufacturing plants and company's headquarters. It also houses the Toyota Automobile Museum, where you can visit an impressive collection of automobiles from throughout the world. One of the highlights of the museum is the Toyota 2000GT, made famous by You Only Live Twice in 1967.

Originally designed by Yamaha, the front-engine, rear-wheel drive, two-seat, hardtop coupé grand tourer was first offered to Nissan, but they declined. Toyota did accept the offer, but had the prototype redesigned by their own designer Satoru Nozaki. The result was Japan's first supercar and only 351 units were ever built.

For collectors the Toyota 2000GT is the most valuable Japanese car

The convertible that is featured in the film was never a production model though. EON Productions commissioned Toyota to build two one-off convertibles, which would enable them to film inside the car as well. One of these two still exists and is on display at the Toyota Museum and is considered one of the museum's most valuable possessions.

Interior of the 2000GT on display at the Toyota museum

The museum's official address is 41-100 Yokomichi, Nagakute City, Aichi Prefecture 480-1118 and it's open every day (except Mondays) between 9.30am and 5pm.

If you travel by Shinkansen, you should get out at Nagoya Station. Then take the metro Higashiyama Line towards the end station Fujigaoka (**H22**), where you should change to the Linimo. The Nagoya Linimo is the only Maglev Linear motor car in Japan and it rides between Fujigaoka and Yakusa. It will bring you to Geidai-dori Station (**L05**) in about 10 minutes. Get out there and follow the signs towards the Toyota Automobile Museum, a ten minute walk.

For more info, please visit **www.toyota.co.jp/Museum/english/**

Sean Connery and Akiko Wakabayashi at Nakano-Shimbashi station

Kinkaku-ji, or the Golden Pavilion, in Kyoto

Kyoto

Kyoto has always played a very important role in Japanese history. It was the centre of the Japanese Empire until decision was made to move the government to Edo (modern Tokyo), in 1868. Although the city has always suffered from wars, fires and earthquakes, it was in fact deliberately spared by the Allied Forces during WW2. Not a single bomb hit the city, which enables today's visitors to find real ancient monuments and temples here.

TOP 5 PLACES TO SEE IN KYOTO

1. **Gion**
   A collection of streets defined by its old wooden buildings, teahouses and exclusive Japanese restaurants, Gion is by far the most famous Geisha district. Spend an hour wandering the area and chances are you'll glimpse a geisha or two shuffling between teahouses in their kimono.

2. **Minokou Restaurant**
   Japanese cuisine doesn't get more refined than *Kyo-ryori*, or "Kyoto cuisine." For the best *Kyo-ryori* experience, head to Gion and the 100-year-old Minokou Restaurant.

3. **Kiyomizu-dera Temple**
   The temple is part of the Historic Monuments of Ancient Kyoto UNESCO World Heritage site and was one of 20 finalists for the *New7Wonders of the World*. It can be really crowded and the approach looks like you're in a market, the stunning view across the city makes up for it.

4. **Kinkaku-ji (or "Golden Pavillion")**
   Kinkaki-ji is a Zen Buddhist temple and one of the most popular buildings in Japan, attracting a large number of visitors annually. The original pavilion dated back to the 14th century, survived WWII, but was burned down in 1950 by a novice monk. The current pavilion is from 1955.

5. **Nijo Jinya**
   Opposite Nijo Castle, this private house is the secret Ninja house Fleming and his friends visited. Expect trap doors, secret passages and much more. Reservations must be made in advance – tours are only in Japanese, unless you hire your own interpreter. (nijyojinya.net/English.html)

Surrounded by hills, Kyoto is a wonderful city to visit and the many beautiful temples and Imperial Palaces can consume a lot of your time. Kyoto remains awash with remnants of its past glory. The city's stunning collection of UNESCO World Heritage sites alone would be enough to set it apart, but Kyoto also boasts a still-working geisha district, some of Japan's most exquisite cuisine and a whole lot of Zen. So I can really recommend spending some time in Kyoto, even though it has no Bond related film locations.

Most foreign visitors arrive in Kyoto by train and the first thing they see is a very modern station. Being part of the train station, the Hotel Granvia is a highly recommendable place to stay. Not quite a traditional or budget hotel, but the service and location make sure this hotel should be on every visitor's list. From the Granvia it's only a few steps to the Shinkansen platforms, from where you can continue your tour.

Nachisan

A very interesting filming location to visit, off the beaten path, is Nachisan. From Kyoto it's 250 to 300 kilometres to Japan's East coast, depending on which route you take. By train it takes you 6 hours, by car it's still at least 3,5 hours. Therefore an overnight stop is highly recommended. Nara, with all its world heritage sites, is probably the most interesting stop option, but Wakayama is closer. From there you should be able to get to Nachisan in a shorter time than mentioned above.

The largest city close to Nachisan is Shingu. Since hardly any western tourists come here, you will notice you are a real attraction and have little children stare and wave at you all the time. Quite a funny experience! From Shingu it's about 10 minutes to the falls by simply following the signs. The Nachi-no-Taki Falls are the highest falls of Japan and rank among the top three most beautiful places to visit.

Once you arrive at the site, park your car on the parking lot and start walking towards the falls. From various platforms you can enjoy the wonderful view before you start your climb to the temple and shrine, located a few hundred meters above you on the mountain.

At the base of the temples you will find two entrance gates, the gate building on your right will bring you to the Buddhist Seiganto-ji temple, while the red Tori on your left brings you to the Kumano-Nachi-Taisha Shinto shrine. Since both buildings were used in YOLT, we will follow the course of the film and start with the Buddhist temple complex. After climbing up the stairs (which you will probably already recognize) you will find yourself on the main square from where you will have an excellent view of the pagoda and waterfall in the distance.

Over the years, buildings have been destroyed and added here (the very large Believer's Hall next to the entrance gate being the most obvious recent addition), so the picture doesn't completely fit the memory you will have from YOLT, but the most important buildings are still here and very recognizable.

The wedding ceremony starts with a view of the bell fry, still here, looking exactly as in 1966. Then the wedding party finds its way to the front of the main temple, the Seiganto-ji. Here, Bond and Tanaka wait for the bride to appear from the stairs you climbed earlier. When, finally, Kissy appears and is introduced to Bond, the party moves on to the neighbouring Kumano Shrine, where the actual wedding ceremony was filmed. The reason for this is unclear. While it might be that filming was not allowed inside the Buddhist Temple, it can also be because the brightly red coloured Shrine simply makes a better picture. Whatever the case, the Kumano Shrine looks fantastic and can be entered by tourists as well. This gives us the opportunity to get close to the place where Bond marries Kissy.

Previous page:
Connery is getting dressed in a traditional wedding kimono

Above:
Connery and Tamba having a break on location at Nachisan

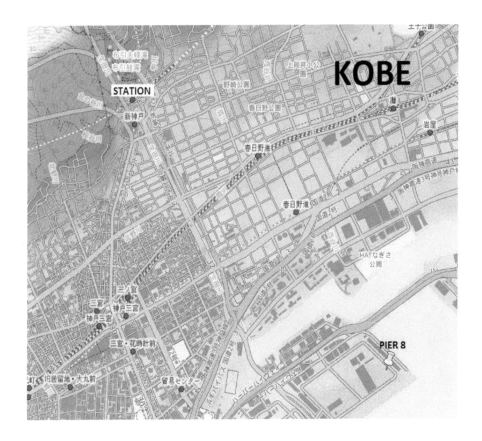

Kobe

Another destination with a Bond connection that can be easily reached from Kyoto, is Kobe. For many years this was Japan's most important port, until disaster struck hard. On January 17th, 1995, Kobe was hit by a major earthquake known as the Great Hanshin Earthquake. 7.3 on the Richter scale, the earthquake killed nearly 6,500 people, leaving more than 300,000 people homeless. Images from the destroyed elevated Hanshin Expressway flew around television screens worldwide, forever linking Kobe to one of the costliest natural disasters in our time.

Kobe's harbour was almost completely destroyed, taking away your only reason to visit the city. Back in 1966 EON took over Pier 8 of the docks to film Bond and Aki looking for the Ning-Po. The subsequent fight scene on the dock and on the roof tops was also filmed here, but nothing has survived the terrible devastation of the Hanshin Earthquake. New piers have been built now, enabling Kobe to slowly regain their top position as a major Japanese port.

At Onohama-cho, an artificial island in the district of Chuo-ku, you can find the location of Pier 8, all the way to the east.

Connery with stand-in Bill Baskerville
on location at Kobe docks, 1966

Himeji

On your way to the south of Japan, the Shinkansen makes only a few stops. One of them is of particular interest for us: Himeji and the Himeji Castle, the best preserved (wooden!) castle in Japan. Recognized by the UNESCO as World Cultural Heritage, this magnificent building dominates the sleepy city and attracts millions of tourists from Japan and overseas every year. Its bright white plastered façade and towers also caught the attention of the EON reconnaissance team while scouting locations in the area. At that time still desperately searching for Fleming's coastal castle, they knew this castle simply had to be used in the film. And it worked very well.

Connery with Tetsuro Tamba on location at Himeji

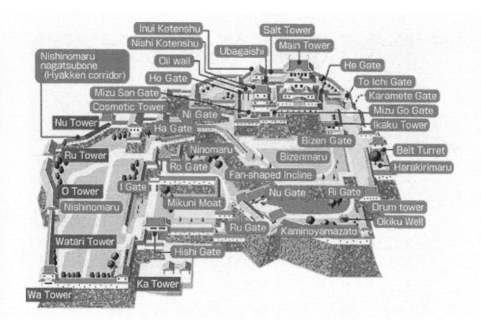

Built around 1600, the wooden structure, nicknamed 'the White Heron' miraculously survived WW2 bombing, enabling EON to use the castle to its fullest capacity in YOLT. The first glimpse we get of Himeji is when Tiger, Aki and 007 land with a chopper on the field in front of the castle. We are then treated on a tour of the castle, while Tiger is showing Bond his ninjas and their training facilities. The clever layout of the ground plan, with its slopes and U-turns (all designed to confuse and slow the enemy down), was shown in the training scenes.

When continuing your way up, you will inevitably climb the slope to the *HA Gate*. This section of the castle was used in the scene where Tanaka explains Bond that he has to become Japanese and marry a Japanese girl to reach the remote island where Blofeld is hiding. After climbing to the top of the castle, the guided course leads to the stone base of the castle structure. The field in front of it is called *Bizenmaru* and can be seen in the training exercise shots.

On the other side you can walk through the Bizen Gate, which will lead to the area where Tanaka's ninja's were practicing their *shuriken* (or throwing stars) techniques.

The slope towards the Ha Gate: Tanaka talks to Bond and Aki

The area leading towards the Ri Gate: Shuriken exercise area

Top: Bizenmaru, where the group training was staged

Right: Connery relaxing in between takes at Himeji Castle

95

Below and next pages: Former U.S. Marine Donn F. Draeger demonstrating techniques en choreographing the training scenes at Himeji Castle with Sean Connery.

Kyushu

Your trip continues southwards, your end goal being Kyushu. This most southern of the larger islands of Japan is attached to the main island of Honshu by a train- and car bridge, so you hardly notice you're actually on a different island. Fukuoka is the Shinkansen's last stop (in fact the last stop is confusingly called *Hakata*, which happens to be the northern part of Fukuoka), from where there are many options to continue your trip further. If you want to explore the rural countryside and exciting things Kyushu has to offer, you should consider travelling to Beppu in the north (famous for its hot springs or *onsen*), like Fleming and his buddies did in 1962.

Nagasaki

Or you could travel to the south/west, where Nagasaki is waiting for you. Together with Hiroshima (which you in fact passed on your way to Kyushu), Nagasaki is ready to teach people an important lesson, by showing the horror caused by the atomic bomb that exploded here on August 9th, 1945.

Being unable to identify the city of Kokura - their initial target - due to poor visibility, the crew of the B-29 bomber *Bock's Car* set course for their alternative target, Nagasaki. They arrived at 10:58am amid heavy cloud and circled around for a short time. Then, a gap in the clouds enabled the crew to identify the Mitsubishi Arms Factory, sealing the fate of the city and its inhabitants. At 11:02am they dropped the bomb *Fat Man*, which had twice the explosive power of the bomb that hit Hiroshima. Seconds later the bomb exploded at an altitude of 500m, directly above the largest Catholic church in Asia, Urakami Cathedral, instantly killing 74.000 people and annihilating the Urukami district. Yet, the damage might have been far worse had the targeted arms factory been hit.

Another place of interest, for a whole different reason, is *Dejima*. It's a fan-shaped piece of land, that used to be in the harbour (but has since been swallowed and surrounded by urban development) and was home to the only foreign trading post that was allowed in Japan for 200 years. After the Portuguese and other Catholic nations were expelled from Japan in 1638, the shogunate ordered the Dutch East India Company (V.O.C.) to transfer its operations from the port of Hirado to Dejima in May 1641. After successfully introducing things like beer, coffee, chocolate and tomatoes, finally in 1857 the Dutch were allowed to leave their island and do their business in Nagasaki and other areas as well.

More recently Nagasaki became interesting for Bond fans, when EON used Hashima (better known as *Gunkanjima* or 'Battleship Island') as the backdrop and model for villain Raoul Silva's hideout in the 2012 Bond film *Skyfall*.

NOT TO MISS IN NAGASAKI:

1. **Atomic Bomb Museum & Hypocentre Park**
   An essential experience, the museum shows the city's destruction and loss of life through photos and artefacts, like a clock that stopped at exactly 11:02am. Chilling.

2. **Dejima**
   Old Dutch trading post, which is preserved as an open-air museum.

3. **Nagasaki ropeway**
   A fantastic way to reach the summit of Mount Inasa and to enjoy some of the most spectacular views of the area.

Hashima is a tiny, deserted island in the East China Sea, some 15 kilometres off the Japanese coast. When coal was discovered on the sea bed in the late 19th century, workers were brought in and out every day to work in the mines. At some point it was decided it would be easier to let them live on the spot, so a small island city was established, complete with school, cinema, pool, restaurants and temples.

During WW2, the island was used for forced labour. This fact was never officially acknowledged, which surely scarred the island's history. In recent years, attempts were made by the Japanese authorities to let the island become a UNESCO World Heritage Site. But this only happened in 2015, after the Japanese hesitantly acknowledged the island's dubious past. The island was re-opened for public visits in 2009.

Swedish film maker Thomas Nordanstad, who made a documentary about the island in 2002, recorded that at some point 5,000 people inhabited the island, making it the most densely populated place on earth, ever. According to the documentary, coal ran out in 1974 and the Mitsubishi Company, who owned the mine, told the people that alternative work was available for them on the mainland, provided on a first come – first served basis. So everyone just took off a.s.a.p., leaving everything behind.

Daniel Craig took notice of the documentary and apparently remembered the island during pre-production meetings for Skyfall. Instead of filming on location, only long distance shots of the island were used, while the abandoned apartment buildings were partly recreated on the studio's back lot and later mixed with CGI effects.

To visit (part of) the island, you will need to book a tour from one of the few official tour companies that are allowed to land on the island. Offices can be found at the Nagasaki port terminal building.

Images on this page and the previous page show the eerie appearance of Hashima Island. The bottom photo on this page shows the U-shaped building that was recreated at Pinewood Studios for *Skyfall*. This area is not accessible for visitors.

Kirishima

All Kyushu's Bond locations are in the south, mostly around Kagoshima, so if that's your priority then just take the train or rent a car and take the expressway towards *Dazaifu* and then *Kumumota*. There, it might be an interesting sidestep to take the 57 eastwards, to Aso and Aso National Park. The town of Aso itself is interesting because you will find yourself in one of the largest active volcanoes in the world. The caldera is 25 km x 18 km wide and it's a strange feeling to find little towns and hotels here. A unique experience is to climb Mount Naka all the way until you reach its highly active crater. A road leads to the top and after leaving the car park, you can walk the last 100 meters to the actual crater. Everywhere you look you will notice concrete shelters or bunkers, put here after a sudden eruption caused the death of some tourists a few years ago. Nowadays, electronic equipment installed inside the crater is being monitored 24/7 and guards with earphones are always in contact with the nearby communications centre, all to quickly evacuate tourists if the circumstances ask for this. The phosphor smell and fumes from the crater itself make a small sign saying "Do Not Enter" on the edge of the crater a little unnecessary, but at least they do warn you..

After a two hour ride by car, you will get to the city of Ebino, where the expressway splits. Here you can go east to Miyazaki (Miyazaki Highway) or west to Kagoshima (Kyushu Highway). A third and probably better option is to enter Ebino and find the small road leading onto the Ebino Plateau, a mountainous region with 5 rather large volcanoes. One of them was used as Blofeld's hidden base in *You Only Live Twice*.

At the Ebino Plateau, there are wonderful hiking paths that can bring you to the tops of all the volcanoes. I personally climbed to the top of Shinmoe-dake (Blofeld's volcano) back in 2006. In the 2008 edition of the book *On the tracks of 007* I wrote a small account of this amazing journey:

> It turned out, there's a really good hiking trail running from the car park all the way to Ebino city, leading over the tops of all five active volcanoes in Kirishima National Park. And the folder

actually clarified some of the distances as it clearly stated it was a full 1 hour climb to the first top, Mount Naka-dake, then another full hour to the second which was my final destination, Mount Shinmoe or Shinmoe-dake, Blofeld's hideout. Then taking into account the fact that we also had to return (meaning another two hours of walking) I started to feel a little worried if we could actually pull this off. The weather was also not really co-operating. It was rather cold, foggy and even rainy up in the mountains, but we decided to give it a try and see where it would take us. And it didn't take us very far that afternoon..

After about 15 minutes we couldn't even see each other because of the dense fog and the rain started pouring every now and then, making it not the pleasant journey I had hoped it would be. We decided to call it a day and returned to the car.

The next day we had only scheduled to drive to Kagoshima, a small hour more to the south, so we fortunately had enough time to give the climb a second try. We took lots of food, crisps, candy bars and water with us, not expecting to come across a food vendor at the top. This was a good idea which would definitely pay off during the following climb and a tip you should not take for granted. We drove to the car park again, put on our shoes (since I'm not really the hiking type we did not have a very professional outfit and totally lacked hiking shoes..) and started walking. It was still a bit foggy but the higher we got the better it became. After a while we left the low clouds behind us and the sun was really burning on our shoulders from then on. (That was another tip: Do NOT forget sun-block, even if you can't see the sun from ground level!)

After a while we got to the foot of the first volcano, Nakadake, where the path just stopped. Apparently it had washed away during heavy rainfall, and we had to climb to the top by jumping from rock to rock, improvising our own road. When we finally reached the top it had taken us 1,5 hours… So much for the information our handy folder! Naka-dake is hardly worth

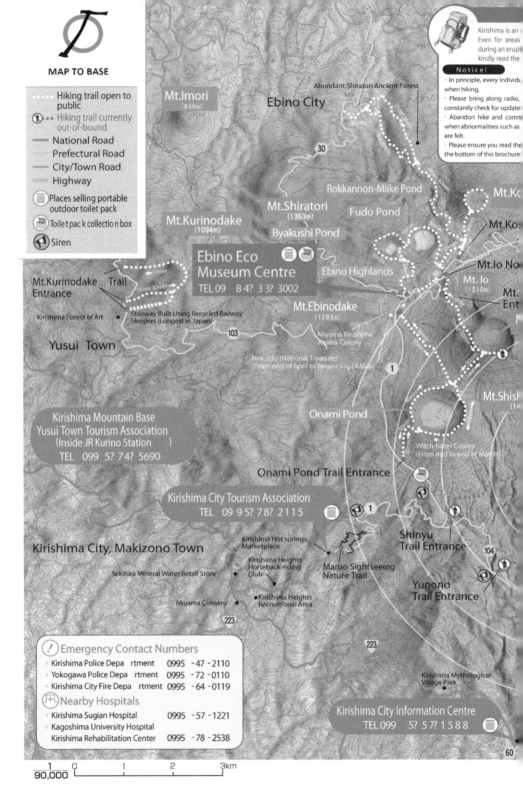

...cano. Do not enter areas which are out-of-bounds.
...re not designated as out-of-bounds, do note that
... can be impending dangers in these areas as well so
... notice and be clear about them before climbing.

...onsible for himself/herself

...hones, compass, etc., to
... directions, weather, etc.,
...scend quickly but calmly,
...kes, earth rumblings, etc.,

...ion and notices below (at

Out of Bounds

Due to the recent activities of Mt.Shinmoedake, the hiking trails leading to Mt.Nakadake (Nakadake) and Mt.Shinmoedake (Shinmoedake), as well as all hiking trails within 2km of Mt.Shinmoedake, are closed. Be sure not to use these trails.

Kobayashi H...

1

• Mt.Hinam...
Entrance

Lake Tour and Nature Trail

Shiratoriyama
Mt.Shiratori (1363m)

Koshikidake
Mt.Koshikidake (1301m)

This two-hour course begins near the Ebino Eco Museum. Going clockwise, one can enjoy the view of three crater lakes - Byakushi Pond (Byakushi-Ike), Rokkannon-Miike Pond (Rokkannon Miike), and Fudo Pond (Fudo-Ike). A steep gradient leads to the summit of Mt.Shiratori, where one can find a shallow crater with a diameter of about 600m, and also enjoy the view of Mt. Sakurajima (to the south) and Mt.Karakunidake. With a large variety of flora, this place is clothed in Kyushu Azalea and verdure in early summer, and filled with beautiful autumn leaves in fall
From the forked road located to the north of Fudo Pond, it takes about 60 minutes one-way to hike up Mt.Koshikidake. In the crater of Mt.Koshikidake lies a plain filled with Susuki grass. The centre portion is a low-rise wetland moor (relatively rare in southern Kyushu), where one can find the carnivores Sundew plant. There is a steep gradient slightly before the summit and the trail become narrower so take note not to lose your way.

dake

ake Trail Entrance

il Entrance

unidake Trail

akunidake
(1700m)

Ohata Pond

Mt.Maruoka
(1330m)

Mt.Hinamoridake
(1344m)

Rokkannon Hall
Mt.Shiratori North Viewing Platform
Mt.Koshikidake
Mt.Shiratori
Rokkannon-Miike Pond
Byakushi Pond
40 min
60 min
Mt.Shiratori Eastern Trail Entrance
To Kobayashi
To Ebino City
30 min
Fudo Pond
Mt. Io North Trail Entrance
30 min
15 min
Ebino Plateau Viewing Platform
10 min
15 min
1310 m Mt. Io
Ebino Eco Museum Centre
Hot spring line
Mt. Io, Daigyou,
Mt.Karakunidake Divergence
1
To Kirishima Hot Springs
To Mt.Karakunidake

Hinamori-dai Camp Ground

Mt.Ohata
(1353m)

At Alert Level 2, the vicinity within 1km from the crater will be closed.

Mt.Shinmoedake
(1421m)

Mt.Yadake
(1132m)

Sano Shrine

1 km

Ouji-baru Park

2 km

Mt.Nakadake
(1332m)

Takaharu Town

Kirishima East Shrine
413

Takachihonomine ridge
(1574m)

Site of old
Kirishima Shrine

3 km

Miike Wild Bird Forest

Takachiho Valley
Campgrounds

Inverted Sword
of the Gods

Koike

Miike

Takachiho Valley Trail Entrance

4 km

Miike Youth Nature House

480

Takachiho
Visitors' Centre
TEL 099 5? 5 7? 2505

5 km

Miyakonojo City

Kirishima City, Kirishima

223
45

ma

Green Village

the climb since it has no crater lake, but the views during the climb are unimaginable. From the top you can even see the city of Kagoshima and the very impressive Sakura-jima volcano in her bay, about 100 kilometres away. Also visible was Shinmoe-dake, luring in the (actually not so far) distance. We had discussed our time problem during the climb and we now had to decide whether we would go on or not. The first part had been a very exhausting climb and we were almost at the point of leaving the plan and return home. At that point I just started walking towards Shinmoe-dake, because it appeared much closer than the 1 hour walk stated in the folder. And this feeling turned out to be correct, it only took us 30 minutes and the climb was a piece of cake compared to the first one. And reaching Shinmoe-dake became one of the highlights of my life..

After a pleasant walk along the edge of Naka-dake and through the valley linking the two volcanoes, a steep but short climb starts, leading to the top of Blofeld's hideout in You Only Live Twice. That first view over the edge you will never forget. The fluorescent green crater lake looks EXACTLY like in the film and it will really take your breath away for a while. Look around you and imagine a full first unit film crew on the edges here. While the director, producers and stars would be flown in by helicopter, the crew actually had to walk its way to the top, like we just did. Using two mules for the heavy equipment this would not have been what everyone expected from exotic location shoots.

We spent a good time at the top, sniffing up the phosphor fumes and looking around, taking lots of photos. The outer rim was clearly the area used to 'hide' Tanaka's ninja's before the final assault on the rocket launching facility beneath the fake lake surface. Of course I couldn't resist throwing a stone in the lake, but mine just sank to the bottom..

After this account of my experience, you probably expect to be encouraged to follow my footsteps. But this is unfortunately not the case, since the area around Mount Shinmoe-dake has been closed off for public since 2011.

Volcanoes are part of Japanese life. They can be found from the northernmost tip to the southernmost tip of the country, making the Japanese archipelago one of the world's most volcanically active. Every now and then one will erupt and sadly that's exactly what happened with Blofeld's HQ.

Shinmoe-dake had erupted before, in the 18th century and more recently in 1991. But the real trouble started in 2008 and 2009, with small eruptions. Then in March 2011, two days after the Tōhoku earthquake and tsunami (which caused the Fukushima nuclear disaster), Shinmoe-dake exploded, robbing us from our beloved green crater lake.

Shinmoe-dake after the 2009 eruption

When you look at satellite images of the area, all you see now is a grey area: Molten stone, mud and lava, in and around the top. For security reasons, a 2 km area around the volcano's top is off limits for hikers until further notice. It's really very sad, but even if the security is lifted, Shinmoe-dake will never again look the way it did when it doubled for the exterior of Blofeld's hidden rocket base in 1966/67.

The skies above the Kirishima mountain range were also used to film parts of the Little Nellie helicopter chase. Unfortunately EON wasn't allowed to have Little Nellie fire rockets here. Additionally, the Japanese pilots had a hard time flying so close to each other and, after Johnny Jordan's accident, it was decided to film the rest of the actual dog fight over the *Sierra de Mijas* mountain range in Spain. Still, it's a beautiful area to drive through and there are still plenty of hiking paths left, so nothing is keeping you from visiting this amazing area.

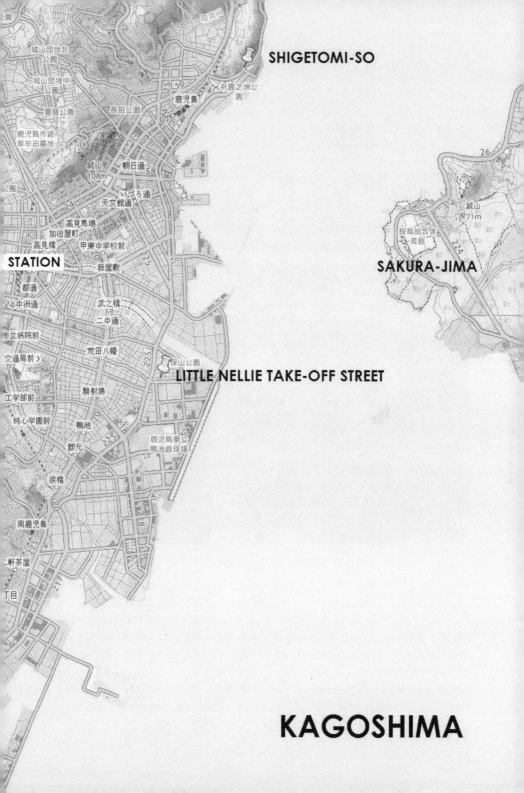

SHIGETOMI-SO

SAKURA-JIMA

STATION

LITTLE NELLIE TAKE-OFF STREET

KAGOSHIMA

Kagoshima

Kagoshima is a medium sized city overlooking Kagoshima Bay, a large bay with a very remarkable feature: In the middle of the bay you will find a huge, active volcano, the Sakura-jima, much like the Italian city of Naples with Mount Vesuvius nearby.

The impressive slopes of Sakura-jima were in fact used in the early stages of the Little Nellie chopper fight. When Bond flies over the island looking for a rocket launching installation, he suddenly spots the shadows of his enemy's choppers on the sides of the volcano. This was filmed above the slopes of Kagoshima's Sakura-jima.

Connery and Wakabayashi surrounded by press in Kagoshima

Kagoshima itself is not very interesting because most of the buildings are post-war and not many authentic spots survived the test of time. Because of its large distance from the rest of Japan, the area is hardly visited by foreign tourists. The place to stay here is the Shiroyama Hotel (formerly known as Castle Park Hotel), overlooking the city. Here the cast and crew stayed while filming in the area, back in 1966. From the hotel the main actors and director were flown to the locations by helicopter, while the rest of the production crew was driven by bus.

This hotel is yet another example of genuine Japanese hospitality which fits in the same list as Tokyo's New Otani and Kyoto's Granvia. The hotel is very recommendable and absolutely worth the extra yen. The view from the hotel of Kagoshima harbour and Sakura-jima is simply breathtaking..

In Kagoshima, you can find two Bond locations. The first one is the road from where Little Nellie takes off. Back in 1966, Kagoshima still consisted mainly of low buildings and more houses than apartments. Nowadays, urban development has changed the look of this city as well, so it took local help to figure out where on earth this scene was filmed.

After Little Nellie has been assembled, Bond takes her for a ride, taking off from a dusty road, apparently behind Tiger's house. This take-off scene was filmed in the centre of the city, in an area called *Tenpozan-cho*, on the road north of the Yojiro Dai 1 Ryokuchi Park. This area has been totally re-developed in recent years, and although the background (Sakura-jima from this angle) matches the film and the street layout has survived, nothing else here will remind you of this scene.

On location in the streets of Kagoshima

Shigetomi-so doubled as the exterior of Tanaka's house

A lot more recognizable is the other location: *Shigetomi-so*. Taking Highway 10 to the north, you will drive through the city for a while, following the signs to *Senganen*, Kagoshima's famous Iso gardens. Just before Highway 10 crosses the Inari River you should take the exit to the right. A small road leads to Tagayama Park. While driving past the park, you will see a small island on your right. After passing the only bridge access to this island (also on your right) you should take the second road on your left. You have now found Shigetomi-so, nowadays one of Kagoshima's most exclusive restaurants and once a villa of the ruling Shimazu clan. It doubled for the exterior of Tiger Tanaka's house.

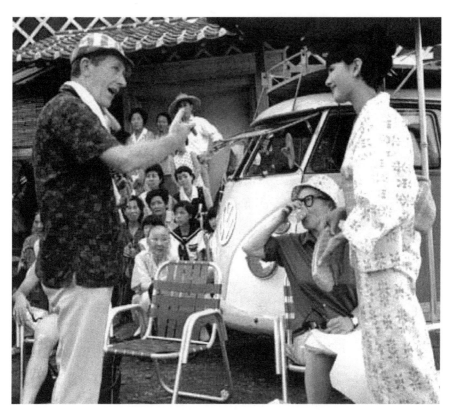

Director Lewis Gilbert enjoys a break with Akiko Wakabayashi

Although no interior scenes were filmed here, the beautiful gardens were used in several scenes. Early in the film, Bond visits Tanaka's house before the bathing scene occurs. We can see Tiger and Bond walk through the garden to the house, the camera looking in the northern direction. Later on in the film, Bond and Aki talk outside in the garden with Tiger about Blofeld's possible hideout, this time the camera looking into southern direction. This scene precedes the one where Q appears and introduces Little Nellie, packed in four heavy suitcases.

Pages 118-119: Behind the scenes at Shigetomi-so

Connery goes for a swim in between takes at Akime. Mie Hama chats with Connery's then-wife Diane Cilento (with sunglasses). Cilento is wearing a black wig, ready to double for Hama, who couldn't swim.

Diane Cilento (front) with Mie Hama at Akime

Akime

One of the possible routes to the tiny town of Akime is a scenic route known as the *Ibusuki Skyline*, offering fantastic views of Kagoshima around every corner. After passing Chiran, a small village with a few ancient samurai houses and landscape gardens as its main tourist attraction, the road splits and you should take the 27 to Makurazaki City. There the road connects with the scenic highway 226 running all along the coast of the Ibusuki Peninsula. Follow this road to the west (your right, keeping the sea on your left) and drive for about an hour and a half.

Akime, although rumoured to be very hard to find, is actually very easy to find. It is mentioned on the road signs, so you actually cannot miss it. There is however another reason you immediately know you're in Akime. The first clue comes from the coastal area, just before you will enter town. A large, round rock in a small bay marks the area where Bond and Kissy supposedly came ashore on their trip to climb Blofeld's volcano.

The biggest clue that you have reached Akime, comes from the fact that EON left a marker outside town: A marble memorial, commemorating the filming that took place here and thanking the people of Akime for their co-operation. This memorial was erected in recent years (1990) and is the only marker ever left by EON at a filming location. Starting with a giant 007 gun logo and followed by the film's name in both English and Japanese, the stone further reads: "*Our James Bond film You Only Live Twice was filmed on location here at Akime*", and bears engraved signatures of Cubby Broccoli, Sean Connery and Tetsuro Tamba.

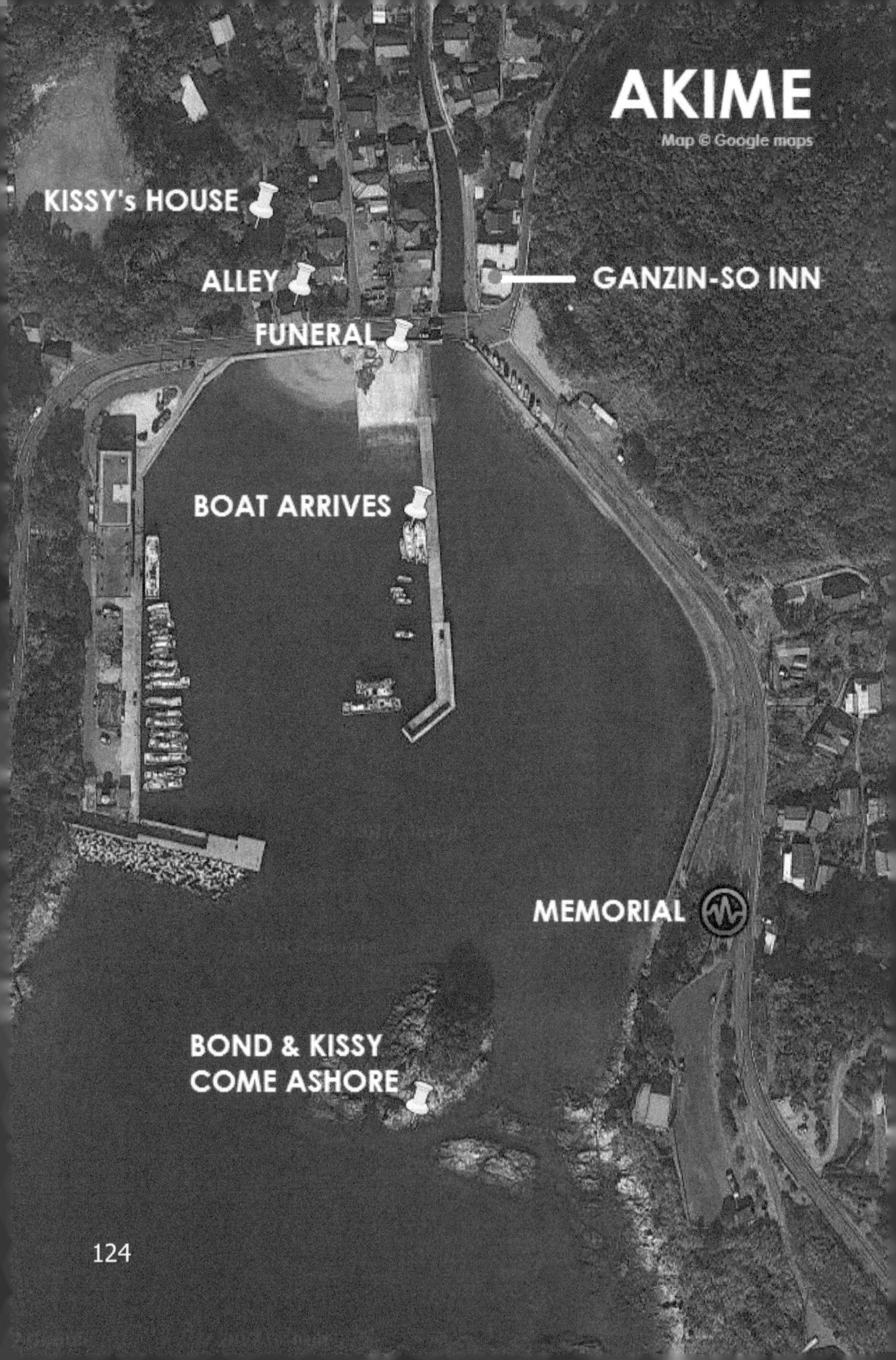

AKIME

Map © Google maps

KISSY's HOUSE

ALLEY

GANZIN-SO INN

FUNERAL

BOAT ARRIVES

MEMORIAL

BOND & KISSY
COME ASHORE

The little fishing village has hardly been touched by foreign influences and actually looks quite similar to the place it portraits in the film, even though it's been more than 50 years ago that a full film crew suddenly put Akime in the centre of world-wide media attention.

The film crew has landed in Akime, as seen from Kissy's house

It must have been a strange phenomenon for the people of Akime. Busloads of equipment and crew members coming in, probably doubling if not tripling the number of inhabitants for two weeks. Suddenly helicopters arrived, bringing in film stars from overseas. A strange toy helicopter made an appearance, and then the busloads of reporters showed up, all trying to catch a glimpse of Sean Connery (to his ever growing frustration). By then, Connery had already had more than enough of all the media attention. He hated the fact that he couldn't enjoy his time in Japan and reacted by making some very unflattering statements about the Japanese, making more enemies than friends.

In fact, one can hardly blame Connery for his reactions considering the fact that some of the most stupid questions were asked during the obligatory press conferences. Reporters were seriously upset when

Connery walked in wearing comfortable clothes, instead of a tuxedo. The Japanese reporter who asked Connery if he was planning on starting his own detective agency deserves special mentioning here.

Tetsuro Tamba at the Ganzin-so Inn

Upon entering Akime, you will find yourself in front of the only restaurant/bar/hotel the town has, the Ganzin-so Inn. During the filming in Akime, this Inn was used to house the main actors. You just HAVE to visit this place. Just enter and politely inform the owners where you come from and why you are visiting Akime. They are so proud of their connection that they will most likely invite you in to see the many photographs they have of the filming. It really is a remarkable collection of official prints and private photos of whatever occurred in that summer of 1966.

When you're outside, facing the inn, just turn left and follow the road along the water. Here Kissy, Bond and Tiger arrived by boat, the latter two posing as locals. They have to wait for the funeral procession to come by, filmed here on this coastal road.

Spectators in Akime observe the filming

Connery and Tamba relax in between takes

After passing a small road on your right you will find the even smaller alley, that leads to the hill above town. When you follow the alley you will end up at a house locally known as *Yamashita's*, the house that was used as Kissy's home. Here Bond and Kissy had dinner and spent the night, overlooking Akime.

Connery had to be guarded to keep fans and press at a safe distance

In Akime's natural harbour the scenes were filmed of the ama girls, the Japanese pearl divers. Exotic Japanese girls had to be brought in for these scenes, because local girls turned out to be too shy to appear in bathing suits. Unfortunately, when filming was about to start it turned out most of them could not swim. Therefore, Diane Cilento, Sean Connery's wife back then, can be seen in some of these scenes, wearing a Japanese wig, diving in the water from the boats.

Top:
Sean Connery having a swim

Left:
Desmond Llewelyn leaning back as a spectator at the Akime shoot

Bottom:
Connery walking towards the Akime beach

Off coast, a large island is visible, Okiakime. Behind this island, unable to see from the coast, lies *Nakabane* Cave, used for the exterior scenes of Bond and Kissy entering the deadly cave. At the end of the film we can see them exiting this cave, followed by Tiger's surviving ninjas. A boat trip to the cave should be arranged on location by just asking someone to take you there, because Akime doesn't operate 007 fan tours to the cave at this stage.. The owner of the Ganzin-so Inn goes there every day though, just so you know.

Filming at Okiakime island and its 'deadly' cave

When filming on Kyushu finished, the plan was to take a plane back to Tokyo, but Connery, bothered by the fact that he still hadn't been able to see a lot of Japan, insisted they'd let him take the train back and so it happened..

Opposite page:
Sean Connery with Mie Hama and in disguise as a Japanese fisherman

This page:
Filming the arrival on the island (top) and the funeral procession (bottom) at Akime harbour

Travelling through Japan is truly a fantastic experience. The Bond locations, although scattered across the country, are marvellous to visit and I can strongly recommend either following this guide or planning your own trip and go see Japan as soon as you can. It will be something you will never forget!

For those of you planning on travelling individually through Japan, here are a few travel tips that might help you:

- The best place to start is Tokyo and then make your way to the south. That way you save the best for last.

- The best time to go is either spring or autumn. The winter can be very cold and the summer is extremely hot and humid.

- While the train is a favourite among most travellers (especially the super-fast Shinkansen bullet trains) I strongly recommend renting a car. Certain remote areas are almost impossible to reach by train and the roads in Japan are very good. Even the smallest town (like Akime) is mentioned in English on the road signs and all rental cars are equipped with a navigation system.

- The well-known car rental companies are present in Japan, but not everywhere. I recommend using either Mazda or Nissan, who run their own rental car agencies and often have an office in or near the train station..

- Avoid one-way car rentals. The return fee is ridiculously high.

- Use the fast Shinkansen for the longer distances between cities, and rent a car in certain areas just for a few days, only to drive around for a few days and return to the city from where you departed. Since rental car agencies usually have offices next to the train stations, you can easily take the Shinkansen to the next city.

- Try to enjoy both the larger, Western style hotels, and the traditional Japanese Ryokans. It is a wonderful experience to have typical Japanese dinner and breakfast in your room, to wait for the maid to make up your traditional Japanese bed and to sleep (very comfortably!) on a futon on the floor.

- Don't expect <u>everyone</u> to speak English. In larger cities you'll be fine, but in rural areas you might encounter people who can only smile at you. Which is nice, but not helping very much.

- Japan is one of the safest countries in the world. People leave their luggage unattended in the middle of a crowded train station to go to the restroom, only to find it untouched when they return.

- The Japanese people are very friendly and helpful. Even when they don't speak your language, they see it as their duty to help you out when you're lost or when you obviously don't know how the subway ticket machine works.

- Prepare your trip well in advance. Large hotels can easily be booked online, using their own websites and booking system, but the ones in smaller towns are hard to find online. Even if they have their own website, it'll be in Japanese. Some very helpful sites for booking hotels or traditional ryokan's are:
  o   http://www.ryokan.or.jp/english/
  o   http://japaneseguesthouses.com/index.htm
  o   http://www.jnto.go.jp/eng/arrange/accomodations/

For more information about visiting the James Bond filming locations, individual trips & guided group tours, please visit

Onthetracksof007.com

Connery goofing around on set and Karin Dor enjoying a photo shoot

Top:
The volcano set under construction at the studio lot

Right:
Filming the bathing scene at Pinewood

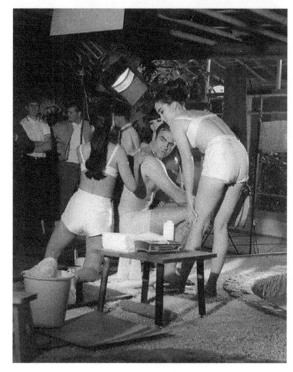

Next page:
Promotional photo shoot with Akiko Wakabayashi

Work in progress: Producer Cubby Broccoli about to place a call, while his EON partner Harry Saltzman goes over the script with writer Roald Dahl.

Lois Maxwell, Akiko Wakabayashi, Sean Connery, Mie Hama and Karin Dor during the press day on Ken Adam's volcano set at Pinewood, October 1966

Connery on the submarine office set, ready for his scenes with Bernard Lee ('M') and Lois Maxwell ('Miss Moneypenny')

Early November '66 D-150 test. Dimension 150 was a brand new widescreen recording method at the time, which would enable filmmakers to shoot wide screen film with an extreme focal range. The above image shows that D-150 was seriously considered as a possible way to fully capture Ken Adam's huge volcano set. It eventually wasn't to be and D-150 died an early death, as only two films were ever filmed using this method.

144

YOU ONLY LIVE TWICE
The filming locations scene by scene

CAPSULE IN SPACE / FLIGHT CONTROL CENTRE
Pinewood Studios, UK

INTERNATIONAL CRISIS MEETING
Control & Reporting Centre Mågerø, Norway

BOND, LING AND THE ASSASSINATION
Pinewood Studios

POLICE CARS ARRIVING
Shan Tung Street, Kowloon, Hong Kong, China

SEA FUNERAL
Aboard HMS Tenby, off coast of Gibraltar

ENEMY AGENT WATCHING WITH BINOCULARS
The Royal Hong Kong Yacht Club, Hong Kong, China

DIVERS GET THE BODY
Bahamas

BOND ABOARD THE SUBMARINE
Pinewood Studios

BOND WITH MONEYPENNY & M
Pinewood Studios

BOND SURFACES IN JAPAN
Okiakime island, off coast Akime, Kyushu, Japan

WELCOME TO TOKYO
Harumi-dori (304) crossing with the 405, Ginza, Tokyo, Japan

BOND GOING INTO THE ALLEY
Suzuran Street, Ginza, Tokyo, Japan

BOND IN THE ALLEY & ENTERS SALON
Miyuki-dori, 5 chome, Ginza, Tokyo, Japan

BOND INSIDE SUMO STADIUM
(ex) Kuramae Kokugikan, Tokyo, Japan - Demolished.

DRIVE TO HENDERSON
Aki's car can be seen driving through West 5th Street and Sotobori-dori, both in Ginza, Tokyo, Japan

ARRIVAL AT HENDERSON'S HOUSE
(ex) Fukuhisa Restaurant, Daiichi-Keihin, 8 chome, Tokyo, Japan
Demolished.

MEETING WITH HENDERSON
Pinewood Studios

FIGHT WITH HENDERSON'S KILLER
Hotel New Otani, 4-1 Kioichō, Chiyoda, Tokyo, Japan

DRIVING THROUGH TOKYO
Azabu-juban, 2 chome – towards Tokyo Tower, Tokyo, Japan

OSATO CHEMICALS (EXTERIOR)
Hotel New Otani, 4-1 Kioichō, Chiyoda, Tokyo, Japan

OSATO CHEMICALS (INTERIOR)
Pinewood Studios

AKI COMES TO THE RESCUE
Hotel New Otani, northern parking lot.

METRO STATION (EXTERIOR & INTERIOR)
Nakano-Shimbashi Metro station, Marunouchi line

TIGER TANAKA'S OFFICE & TRAIN (INTERIOR)
Pinewood Studios

WALKING THROUGH TANAKA'S GARDEN
Shigetomi-so, Kagoshima, Kyushu, Japan

BATHING SCENE
Pinewood Studios

CAR CHASE THROUGH TOKYO:
Hotel New Otani, (ex) southern exit

Road east of Hotel New Otani, towards Benkeibashi

Akasake, 6 chome, street on west side of block 12, Tokyo, Japan

Akasake, 6 chome, street on south side of block 12, Tokyo, Japan

Higashi, street between 2 chome and 3 chome, Tokyo, Japan

Akasake, 6 chome, street on south side of block 18, Tokyo, Japan

Akasake, 6 chome, street on west side of block 18, Tokyo, Japan

Komazawa-dori, in front of the Olympic Stadium, Tokyo, Japan

South side of Yoyogi National Stadium, Tokyo, Japan

BLACK SEDAN PICKED UP WITH MAGNET
Fuji Speedway, Oyama, Shizuoka, Japan (east side)

A DROP IN THE OCEAN
Tokyo Harbour

BOND AND AKI CHECK OUT THE NING-PO
(ex) Pier 8, Kobe docks, Kobe, Japan - Demolished

INSIDE THE CABIN ON THE NING-PO
Pinewood Studios

PLANE TAKE-OFF AND CRASH LANDING
(ex-) RAF Finmere / Finmere Aerodrome, Buckinghamshire, UK

BRIEFING AT TANAKA'S GARDEN
Shigetomi-so, Kagoshima, Japan

ASSEMBLING LITTLE NELLIE
Pinewood Studios

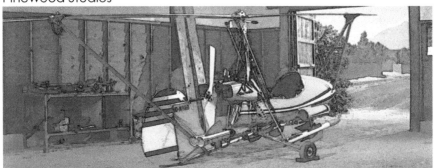

LITTLE NELLIE TAKES OFF
Tenpozan-cho, Ryokuchi Park, Kagoshima, Japan

LITTLE NELLIE FLIES OVER THE FISHING VILLAGE
Akime, Minamisatsuma, Japan

"THERE'S NOTHING HERE BUT VOLCANOES"
Kirishima National Park, Kyushu, Japan

CHOPPERS APPEAR
Mount Sakura-jima, Kagoshima bay, Japan

AERIAL DOGFIGHT
Kirishima National Park, Kyushu, Japan

and Sierra de Mijas, Andalucía, Spain

BLOFELD'S VOLCANO (EXTERIOR)
Mount Shinmoe-dake, Kirishima National Park, Kyushu, Japan

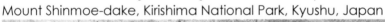

BLOFELD'S VOLCANO (INTERIOR)
Pinewood Studios

PENTAGON MEETING
Pinewood Studios

NINJA TRAINING SCHOOL (EXTERIOR)
Himeji Castle, Himeji, Japan

NINJA TRAINING SCHOOL (INTERIOR)
Pinewood Studios

BOND BECOMES JAPANESE
Pinewood Studios

DEATH OF AKI
Pinewood Studios

BOND KILLS HIS ATTACKER DURING NINJA TRAINING
Hotel New Otani garden, Tokyo, Japan

WEDDING CEREMONY
Nachisan, Natchikatsuura, Wakayama pref. ,Japan

ARRIVAL ON THE ISLAND
Akime, Minamisatsuma, Kyushu, Japan

KISSY's HOUSE ON THE ISLAND
Yamashita's, Akime, Minamisatsuma, Kyushu, Japan

THE DEADLY CAVE
Nakabane Cave, Okiakime island, Kyushu, Japan

BOND AND KISSY COME ASHORE
Akime harbour, Minamisatsuma, Kyushu, Japan

BOND AND KISSY PASS A WATERFALL
Maruo Falls, Kirishima, Japan

REST ON THE MOUNTAIN
Mount Shinmoedake, Kirishima, Kyushu, Japan

PLANES DROP THE RAFTS
Bermuda

BOND, KISSY AND THE NINJAS CLIMB INTO THE RAFTS
Off coast Okiakime Island, Kyushu, Japan

BOND AND KISSY WATCH THE VOLCANO EXPLODE
Pinewood Studios

RAFT PICKED UP BY SUBMARINE
HMS Aeneas, off coast Gibraltar

Also available:

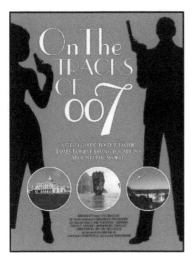

ON THE TRACKS OF OO7 -
a field guide to the exotic James Bond
filming locations around the world

ISBN 978-90-813294-1-5 (B/W)
ISBN 978-90-813294-2-2 (Colour)

Written by: M. Mulder / D. Kloosterboer
Published in: 2008

On the tracks of 007 is the ultimate field
guide to the Bond locations, covering
all the locations from Dr. No (1962) to
Quantum of Solace (2008)

Available at **Onthetracksof007.com**

大里化学工学

OSATO CHEMICALS ENGINEERING CO. LTD.
4-1 Kioicho, Chiyoda, Tokyo 102-8578, Japan

New Otani 1966

New Otani 2017

ABOUT THE AUTHOR:

Martijn Mulder ('71) is a freelance writer, who lives in the Netherlands. His website about the 007 filming locations is one of the longest running James Bond related sites, being online since 1995. Together with Dirk Kloosterboer, Mulder wrote the travel guide **On the tracks of 007**, which was published in 2008. He frequently organises trips and guided tours to the filming locations around the world.

Image credits:

Pages 13, 14, 23, 63, 66, 67, 69, 71, 79, 85, 86, 87, 94, 95 (top), 99, 104, 105, 116, 122, 123 © Martijn Mulder, Pages 51-53 & 96-98 © Chic Eather
1966-1967 YOLT stills © 007 Location Archive, page 170 © 007 Magazine & Archive
Screenshots by DMD - used for reference only © Danjaq LLC, UA / MGM
Cover illustration by Jeffrey Marshall
Drawing on page 27 by Sir Ken Adam
Maps OSM (TF landscape) © Martijn Mulder
Map pages 108-109 © Kirishima Trekking Map, page 124 © Google Maps
Other images: Wikimedia Commons

Special thanks to:

Jeffrey Marshall, Norman Wanstall, Shinichi Murai, Yoshi Nakayama, Uwe Brosamle, Thomas Gleitsmann, Frank Anderson, Steve Oxenrider and Graham Rye

For more information:

To contact the author, please send an e-mail to **info@onthetracksof007.com** or visit the website: **www.onthetracksof007.com**